THE EFFECTIVE COMMUNICATION METHOD

9 KEYS TO MASTER COMMUNICATION SKILLS

THE COMPREHENSIVE TRAINING GUIDE TO STEP BY STEP IMPROVE YOUR COMMUNICATION SKILLS AND BUILD SUCCESSFUL RELATIONSHIPS

BRIAN BASTERFIELD

D1293933

SelfGrowth
365

To my wife and my son

who always encouraged me!

CONTENTS

A FREE GIFT TO THE READERS

Thank you for reading *The Effective Communication Method*.
I hope you will find it insightful and practical.
To help you get the best results I have included the following additional
material that no extra cost to you:

This is a quick guide to managing your emotions that plays an
important role in communications.
To get your additional material please scan the QR code below:

INTRODUCTION

A decade ago, if you'd told me I'd be writing a book about communication skills, I would have laughed in your face and told you to look for something more relevant. But the fact is that life is full of surprises. In a world where almost no one knows how to communicate well with other people, I feel it is essential to know the communication method and use it to build relationships.

I had the fortune of being close to many entrepreneurs who were successful in their fields, but success does not necessarily mean that we communicate well.

According to the National Institute of Mental Health, 73% of the population is afraid of communicating in public. Now, this is not necessarily public speaking to a large crowd, but rather just speaking in a public setting where others may hear them.

Some people get stuck in the same patterns of communication all their lives and never know how to change or improve. Your perception of the world and your ability to communicate with others is shaped from the moment you are born, so the sooner you grasp this, the better off you will be in the future.

If you're reading this book, you're probably feeling something similar. You probably don't know how to proceed when a conversation isn't going well. Awkward silences, sudden changes in subject, and agreeing to things we don't want to agree with to end the conversation are all coping mechanisms that help us limp through bad conversations but ultimately leave us feeling confused, embarrassed, or frustrated.

My life began in a challenging environment, and my younger years were marred by depression and anxiety. This experience proved to be the catalyst for a lifelong interest in personal growth and development. Determined to turn things around, I made self-development my goal, leading to an ongoing interest in human behavior and psychology. That's when I realized that communication is the key to success. If you know how to communicate with people properly, that's when success will follow.

In this book, which is the result of my academic research and personal life experience, you will learn to:

- Know yourself and your environment so that you can optimize the relationships within it
- Listen and don't just hear people
- Be aware of your language
- Pay attention and communicate using non-verbal cues
- The role of empathy in communication
- How to handle emotions

Some of the people I have academically researched over the years of writing self-improvement include the famous Mahatma Gandhi, Thomas Jefferson, and Abraham Lincoln.

Abraham Lincoln missed out on an important opportunity to speak at a Republican-led political committee in New Jersey due to being anxious about speaking.

As a public figure, Mahatma Gandhi felt the strain of speaking was such a burden that he even avoided it during intimate dinner parties and friendly get-togethers. His first court case was a communication disaster because he was so anxious that he panicked and fled the courtroom after managing only one sentence.

Thomas Jefferson was so afraid of speaking to others, even after becoming the third president of the United States and a Founding Father, that he was diagnosed with social phobia. John Adams, the 2nd president of the United States, claimed he never heard Jefferson speak more than three sentences together the whole time they served together in congress. Ironically, maybe to hide his fear of speaking, Thomas Jefferson famously said,

> *"The most valuable talent is that of never using two words when one will do."*

— **THOMAS JEFFERSON**

This shows that fear of communication permeates the highest echelons of society. You and I are no exception to the norm.

Interestingly, all the above (and many others) that I have studied overcame their fear of verbal communication with exceptional written communication. And in this book, I have dedicated an entire chapter to mastering written communication.

We can all do something to change the course of our communication paths. Most of the people who have become excellent communicators started with poor skills.

Fear of public speaking is ranked as the number one phobia in America. My book will help you overcome this fear that has so many people in its grip with practical lessons and examples. I have implemented the combination of topics I share with you, and they have worked for me and many others that have shared their success with me.

> *"People fail to get along because they fear each other; they fear each other because they don't know each other; they don't know each other because they have not communicated with each other."*
>
> **— MARTIN LUTHER KING**

Let's get started on this journey to communicate!

1

TO BE OK, OR NOT TO BE OK: THAT IS THE QUESTION

C ommunication can make you feel OK or not OK. But you have to learn to communicate in the first place to feel anything. Understanding communication is the key to learning how to do it well.

WHAT IS COMMUNICATION?

Communication is the process of exchanging information verbally and in written form. Using communication, you transfer information from one person to another. But this process can be affected by many things, including

- Our emotions
- Our medium of communication

- Our location
- Our cultural situation

Typically, communication has three essential parts, the sender, the receiver, and the message. The sender encodes the message either verbally, in written form, or both and then transmits it to the recipient, who decodes it to get the meaning behind the message.

Face-to-face communication is less complex than non-face-to-face communication.

The sender and recipient can see each other in real-time and react to verbal and non-verbal cues of communication without delay. Because of this, misunderstanding can occur at any point in communication, as the sender encodes a message one way, and the recipient decodes it differently.

Example:

I may pay a compliment to a co-worker by saying:

"You look great in that outfit today, Susan."

And depending on where Susan is emotionally, she may take it as a simple, good-hearted compliment or start asking herself:

"Does he mean I don't look great in this outfit on other days?" or "What's wrong with my other outfits?"

We have communicated, but not effectively.

Effective communication should minimize the potential for misunderstanding among the communicating parties and seek some feedback from the recipient.

TYPES OF COMMUNICATION

- Written communication
- Verbal communication
- Non-verbal communication

All three types of communication are essential to everyday life.

Why Do We Need to Communicate?

To Boost Innovation and Share Information

When we keep the knowledge to ourselves and do not share it, it becomes worthless. But communicating our ideas and thoughts with others helps improve innovation. Sharing information also helps to improve our thinking strategies and creativity.

To Build Relationships

Communication is critical in any relationship. There cannot be a relationship without communication.

When we communicate with each other, we build a connection and trust. But for communication to work in this case, there must also be listening. If you are not heard when you communicate, it becomes impossible to build a lasting, meaningful relationship.

To Develop Personality

Communication is a requirement to let others know your likes and dislikes. When others know about your preferences and dislikes, you can better navigate your world without getting offended or offending others.

Also, communicating helps you explore and work through new challenges due to meeting new people with different personalities, experiences, and views. Communicating with a diverse group of people can be quite helpful for improving communication.

To Resolve Conflicts

Without communication, it is impossible to resolve conflicts. We must talk to each other to reach a consensus and rebuild understanding. When communicating, we also get better knowledge and insight into the other person, which can better the relationship.

As you resolve conflicts, you also express your personal preferences and ideas that help the other person understand your relationship needs.

To Stand Out from the Crowd

Great communication sets you apart as a leader as you express yourself. Most people are happy to recede into the background, so communicators stand out from the crowd. Think of all the great orators you know; don't they stand out from the crowd?

- Winston Churchill
- Cicero
- Barack Obama
- Martin Luther King Junior
- Edward Everett
- Mahatma Gandhi
- Franklin Roosevelt
- Maya Angelou
- Nelson Mandela
- Malala Yousafzai

To Express Decisions

We all have boundaries, but when we meet new people (which we do in everyday activities), they do not know our boundaries. Communication informs others of our boundaries as we express what is acceptable and not acceptable to us. Communicating with others lets them know what we are thinking and our decisions regarding various situations. Also, communicating helps you get advice from others, which influences the eventual decision.

OUTLOOKS ON LIFE AND HOW THEY AFFECT OUR COMMUNICATION STYLE

The Supernatural Outlook

This outlook views life from a supernatural perspective, meaning we look at life through a spiritual lens. That means finding God (or a higher power) in all that happens in life. This affects our communication style by giving us confidence in expressing our doubts and fears with faith that they could come true. When we feel confident, we feel empowered; empowered people are great communicators.

The belief in a higher power takes away the fear that holds us back from expressing ourselves.

The Subjective Naturalism Outlook

This outlook believes life can be meaningful even without God, an afterlife, or the transcendent realm that believers believe in. That affects the communication style by giving us utmost belief in ourselves and our ability to speak and act on our behalf. Such people are great communicators because they know they are their own best advocates.

The belief in a meaningful personal existence makes us more confident and excellent communicators.

The Objective Naturalism Outlook

This outlook believes that life can be meaningful and devoid of infinite or finite influences, unlike subjective naturalism, which believes life can be meaningful without God, but the belief of God I (or a higher power) is present. It also affects our communication style by giving us the confidence to advocate for ourselves.

The belief in a meaningful existence gives us self-reliance and confidence to know we are OK with the universe. That knowledge helps us become objective and confident communicators as we don't rely on a higher power to speak for them or to perform a miracle on their behalf.

The Hybrid Naturalism Outlook

This combination of subjective and objective naturalism allows you to enjoy the best of both worlds. When you know that you can rely on yourself and also on a higher being should you need to, you are confident that one way or another, you will be fine. That gives you the confidence to communicate with others without fear.

The Pessimistic Naturalism Outlook

Unlike all the above optimistic outlooks, this is the only one that is pessimistic. This outlook views life as devoid of meaning because nothing has value. When we approach life seeing everything as lacking value, we end up without an appreciation of the value of others. And without an appreciation of others, there is no desire to communicate with them. Pessimism kills communication.

Apart from the outlooks, there are life positions we tend to take that affect how we communicate. There are four life positions that also affect our communication:

- I'm not OK – You're OK
- I'm OK – You're not OK
- I'm not OK – You're not OK
- I'm OK – You're OK

1. I'm not OK – You're OK (the depressive communication position)

This is where the sender of the message feels they are at a disadvantage because whatever they say has no impact. Their words are futile against the recipient of the message.

Children tend to feel like this when communicating with adults. It is also present in employee-employer scenarios where employees feel they have no say in their work situations.

The recipient of the message is the authority and holds all the power, while the sender is at their mercy.

This communication position is characterized by low self-esteem, feelings of powerlessness, and people-pleasing. It is very childlike, and in most cases, it is developed in childhood when a child encounters bullies, dominant parents, teachers, and peers.

We find ourselves in this position in childhood where the adults in our lives are wiser, stronger, and more knowledgeable than us. But as we grow up, we must break out of this and draw on our self-knowledge and confidence.

Example:

An employee is asking for a raise from the owner of the company. The employee is sending out a verbal/written plea that they are not OK to the recipient, the employer, who holds the ability to make a difference. The employer is in a better position to implement change than the employee.

The employee is not OK – the employer is OK.

If the employer is inconsiderate in their communication with the employee, the latter withdraws back to the child with dominant people in their life that don't listen. It takes a lot for people in this position to communicate because they have a very fragile perception of themselves and get easily depressed by negative responses.

If we communicate from this perspective, we constantly feel inadequate and wrong, which brings shame and embarrassment. Once these feelings take over, communication becomes difficult, and we behave passively.

This is unbridled obedience toward anyone you are communicating with. You tend to feel like the underdog when communicating with everyone, automatically elevating the other person.

2. I'm OK – You're not OK (*The paranoid communication position*)

The sender feels like they are OK and doing well, almost in a position of superiority over the recipient. The verbal or written communication from the sender tends to be bossy and callous, using bragging language and boasting of their achievement.

Many insecure people tend to adopt this type of communication position to feel like they fit in. Their communication style can come across as abrasive and superior.

Example:

An employer is responding to an employee's request for a raise. They call the employee to the office and ask them disparaging questions about their education level, private life, and ambitions. The communication features statements and questions like:

"How do you expect a raise when you have never been to college? I have three degrees; that's why I make the amount of money I do."

"How do you live in such a terrible neighborhood and survive? I couldn't. I have lived in the suburbs all my life and am even considering moving to a completely gated community."

"I am not sure your level of education can help you achieve the goals you have written down here.

"From experience working with many people of your ilk, I am telling you that you will never go further than you are right now. This is the best you can do."

Some people who use this type of communication come from a very passive background, so they try to assert themselves in adulthood.

This is aggressive communication.

3. I'm not OK –You're not OK (The futile communication position)

This is the communication between two people who cannot help each other because they believe in their mutual badness. They cannot take advice because they do not believe the other person has the moral authority to dispense it. This communication is based on isolation or vindictiveness.

It is commonly exhibited in toxic workplaces where employees are pitted against each other.

Example:

Two employees are vying for the same position. They each say things about each other to get the position.

They may tell the employer, "If you are thinking of giving Mr. P the position, he is even worse than me."

Communication doesn't build, and each person feels even more isolated than before. Some people tap out of this environment and become isolated, while others become even more vindictive and graduate to the aggressive communication level.

This is chaotic, destructive communication.

4. I'm OK – You're OK

This is the ideal communication where the exchange of information is positive, empowering, and uplifting. The sender and recipient of the message mutually benefit by building each other up with their communication.

To attain this level of communication, we must be at peace with ourselves which comes after self-analysis. In this communication, we acknowledge the following truths:

- I am OK with myself as you are OK with yourself
- I have shortcomings as you have shortcomings
- I am knowledgeable as you are knowledgeable
- I am good at certain things, and you are good at certain things

We all come with baggage that makes us vulnerable, but that doesn't diminish us, and we do not intend to hurt each other with that knowledge.

Example:

Two people meet at a party and get to know each other through conversation. They have mutual respect and interest in each other, so they speak to each other and not at each other. They get to know each other and build a bond and friendship based on trust and appreciation.

This is harmonious, self-reflective, and appreciative communication.

The fourth position is the best, because it is key to effective communication. But it is cultivated over time and with certain cognition that we explore below:

- **Explore and Analyze Our Memories**

We need to explore and analyze our earliest memories of communication. The brain features a region (the temporal cortex) responsible for our memories and emotions. Triggering a memory helps us relive that experience, and we can begin to explore why we may have communication baggage.

For example, think of childhood words that make you feel melancholic, sad, aggressive, or timid. For some people, words like "you are stupid" or "don't be stupid" trigger memories of a parent communicating harshly with them.

But remind yourself that you are not stupid and you have a brain that functions very well. Own your reality and communicate with your reality in mind. Your reality is that you are not stupid, so speak to others in a knowledgeable manner and with confidence in your information.

• Look Out for Repetition of Old Patterns

We tend to fall back into old patterns when scared or intimidated. Look out for old, poor patterns that seem to rear their head when communicating, like withdrawing when someone asks a personal question, getting agitated when talking about your childhood, or becoming rigid about certain subjects. We swear never to fall back into this habit, but we can get triggered, so be aware.

I am not saying don't be passionate; just do not let your past negative communication patterns take over and rob you of a great conversation with others. Negative communication patterns include aggression, withdrawal, timidity, and insults.

- **Learn to Identify the Moments when Your Inner Child Appears**

Many of us revert to our inner child when confronted with situations we don't like. We not only act like a child but also communicate as one. In these moments, we are not effective communicators.

Be self-aware and recognize those moments when you slip into your inner child and compromise your ability to communicate.

Childlike communication entails rolling your eyes, sulking, tantrums, and explosive reactions. When you feel like acting out in this manner, it means you are not in the "I'm OK – you're OK" zone of communication. You are in the "I'm not OK – you're OK" zone. Breathe in deeply and out slowly until you can feel the inner child receding and a mature response beginning to form in your mind.

- **Recognize Moments of Suppression and Contamination**

Some people may try to suppress you as you communicate. Avoid such people because they are not good for your communication growth. Communication is a two-way street. As you show respect and interest in your communication, it should be reciprocated by the other person.

Also, some people try to contaminate the communication pool by using unhelpful, disrespectful approaches like talking over people. This may be in the hope of drawing you into a yelling match. While yelling is a form of communication, it is not constructive or building.

When yelling, we cannot hear each other over the raised voices, and as such, we cannot respond maturely. All we are doing through yelling is defending our viewpoints, and not acknowledging each other's perspectives.

But many other things can contaminate your communication, like:

- Listening to gossip, which gives you negative connotations about others

- Allowing insults and curse words to permeate your speech to other people

- Allowing stereotypes and racial biases to govern how you communicate with others

We all have an outlook on life that falls into these five categories:

- The Supernatural Outlook
- The Subjective Naturalism Outlook
- The Objective Naturalism Outlook
- The Hybrid Naturalism Outlook
- The Pessimistic Naturalism Outlook

Our communication patterns also fall into the following categories

- I'm not OK - You're OK
- I'm OK - You're not OK
- I'm not OK - You're not OK
- I'm OK - You're OK

When communicating with anyone, it is critical to be aware of your emotional and mental state.

Do not get involved in suppressive communication, because it kills the other person's confidence (and don't allow it to be done to you).

Avoid communication contaminants like gossip, insulting words, and curse words.

2

TURN YOUR AWARENESS ON

W e have to understand awareness to stay in tune with it. So, what is awareness?

Awareness is the state of being perceptive about ourselves.

> *"Your own self-realization is the greatest service you can render the world."*
>
> **— RAMANA MAHARSHI**

In this case, we need to be aware of what is going on in our minds and how it reflects in our communication. Most of our actions are done in a state of unconscious awareness, which translates to how we communicate.

There are two states of awareness.

Conscious awareness: This is a state where the mind is awake and mindful of its communication.

Unconscious awareness: This is where emotions and thoughts outside our awareness continually influence our communication. In unconscious awareness lies repressed feelings, bad habits, negative thoughts, hidden memories, and unfulfilled reactions and desires.

CONSCIOUS AWARENESS AND COMMUNICATION

A combination of conscious awareness and communication results in conscious communication. This is our ability to precisely and compassionately communicate with others because we are thinking wisely. The wisdom in our communication comes from clarity due to silencing the nonstop chatter that goes on in our minds.

Conscious communication allows us to communicate with others calmly and maturely without reacting with a fight-or-flight response. Learning conscious communication will help us reduce stress while communicating and improve our relationships.

Steps to Improve Conscious Communication

Step One: Explore What Happened

When something happens, that requires communication, begin by exploring what happened. Understanding what happened helps you understand the issue's genesis and how to navigate communication.

Take a few deep breaths to help you calm down and refocus on the actual event. Try to look at the moment as a third party and describe as much detail in the third person to help you feel grounded. Exploring what happened can make you relive the emotions that you felt at the time. Count until ten to bring you back to the present moment and calm you down.

Step Two: Explore How You Are Feeling

Name your feelings at that moment and be as descriptive as possible. But avoid words that pronounce victimization.

— DON'TS:

Avoid using words like I feel cheated, abandoned, manipulated, unwanted, betrayed, used, or unappreciated.

✛ DOS:

Make statements like "I feel that I am not receiving the attention I need right now" or "I would like to feel accepted in this conversation, but I don't feel that."

When exploring how you are feeling, focus your description on the four fundamental human needs:

- The need for attention
- The need for acceptance
- The need for affection
- The need for appreciation

Step Three: What Am I Asking For?

Identify and name the specific actions, communication, or behaviors that you are looking for to resolve the issue at hand. But even as you outline these, remember that the person you are communicating with is human, and they may not see things from your perspective. Be open to explaining why you feel as you do and maintain a state of calmness even as you observe the other person's reaction.

With conscious communication, no matter how the situation unfolds, you are aware of the experience you want and what you learn from it. So even if the other person becomes agitated, you remain calm and non-judgmental of their behavior. Maintaining your cool may help the other person also become less agitated, and you can have a mature, calm conversation.

Step Four: What Did You Learn From the Experience?

Having an in-depth look at the experience and drawing helpful lessons from it is critical. You may have a win-win situation where the other person sees your point, and you amicably resolve the issue. This is known as a growing moment. The alternative is where the other person doesn't see your point, and you have a disagreement, but you eventually reach a consensus and find a middle ground (or not). Either way, it is a growing experience.

At this point, it is important to say that even when we understand how conscious communication is supposed to work, it takes time and patience to grow this skill.

Skills to Aid with Conscious Communication

Speak calmly

When we raise our voices, we initiate conflict while staying calm can avert conflict. Our calmness keeps the connection going with the other person, which maintains communication. As mentioned earlier, taking deep breaths helps to ground us and keep us focused on the main issue.

Practice what to say

To speak calmly, we must think about the conversation before having it. That prevents us from reacting to what other people say and instead calmly leads the tone of the conversation.

It is always important to practice what you want to say out loud to catch words that may fuel the flames or work on your tone. Some people start by speaking softly, but as they become emotional, they become louder and more agitated. If that is the case with you, practicing what you will say helps you to remain calm and maintain an even tone as you speak.

Don't pose a question in a statement

This makes us sound unsure. For example, my introduction to a conversation with a person I've had a disagreement with is to establish the facts of what happened. So I say:

> *"I know what the problem is, and you know what the problem is. Now I want us to get past this, and this conversation is critical for us to do that."*

I say this with an even tone while looking the person in the eye so they can read my expression. I do not make faces or show an attitude.

Now, imagine if I had posed a question in my introduction instead of making the statement:

> *"I know you, and I know the problem, right? So let's have this conversation and get over the problem."*

Here the first question appears to make me sound vulnerable, almost like I am looking for approval from the other person to agree about what the problem is. If I want this conversation to be in the "I'm OK – you're OK" zone, the other person should be your equal. In this case, it appears to be more in the "I'm not OK – You're OK" zone.

Slow Down

To consciously communicate, we need to speak slowly and articulate our words so that the other person can hear clearly. Some of our disagreements are because people may not understand what we are saying. Slowing down allows us to pronounce our words correctly.

Also, slowing down helps the other person remain calm by demonstrating that we are not nervous. Nervous energy can be transferred from one person to another, making the conversation awkward and unproductive.

Using our hands helps us to slow down and also speak calmly. But try to keep gestures contained to ensure they do not reflect nervous energy. For example, do not straighten or pick at the table cloth and move the salt and pepper shakers and also don't touch your hair or straighten your clothes which conveys a lack of confidence or nervousness.

Avoid Useless Prefaces

Get right to the point of the conversation. We sometimes use useless prefaces like "Well" or "I mean" to begin sentences. We also like to use caveats in an attempt to explain ourselves, even before the conversation starts. Caveats include starting the conversation with, "Sorry" or "This is just my opinion." These two phrases damage the confidence we are trying to exude during the conversation, instead making us look like we have something to hide.

Consider the two statements below:

1. We should have this conversation in a more neutral setting.
2. I mean, I guess we should have this conversation in a more neutral setting.

Number one gets straight to the point and exudes confidence, while number 2 is apologetic about where the meeting is currently being held.

Insert a Smile

It can be very difficult to want to smile while in the middle of a hard conversation. But try injecting a smile into your voice when you can see the conversation going positively. That will encourage the other person to relax, and they can be more receptive to what you are saying.

But if you are going to smile, make sure it is genuine. If you don't feel like smiling, don't. A fake smile makes you seem disingenuous and puts the other person on edge about you. If you want to appear approachable to the other person, consider smiling as they approach you or as you approach them.

UNCONSCIOUS COMMUNICATION

According to Sigmund Freud's psychoanalytic theory of personality, our unconscious mind is a reservoir of memories, emotions, urges, and thoughts that are outside our conscious self. That means being in the unconscious unleashes unpleasant feelings and behaviors, which are reflected in unconscious communication.

It is believed that conscious communication covers the tip of the iceberg, while unconscious communication covers the undetected lower tip of the iceberg. These feelings that linger underneath the surface cause:

- Anger
- Difficulty in forgiving
- Bias
- Compulsive behaviors

Freud also believed that our basic urges and instincts are all contained in the unconscious mind. Normal unconscious human instincts are related to life and/or death. For example, sexual instincts are basic urges, and they are also life instincts. Also, the instinctive fight-or-flight reaction is in response to the preservation of life, because we all want to survive.

Types of unconscious communication

- Interpersonal unconscious communication
- Intrapersonal unconscious communication

Interpersonal Unconscious Communication

This is unconscious communication between two or more people, so it tends to be more varied than intrapersonal unconscious communication. The sender of the message communicates unconsciously through voice inflection, unguarded speech, stuttering, and high pitch. A normally eloquent and articulate person may unconsciously communicate nervousness, fear, and lack of confidence with the above covert messages.

Intrapersonal Unconscious Communication

Intrapersonal unconscious communication is between a person and themselves. This is unconscious communication occurring in your mind, like dreaming, hypnosis, or memories. For example, a person may be affected by hearing a lullaby, not knowing the song is familiar because they heard it from their mother when she sang it to them as a baby.

Unfortunately, the non-verbal cues in unconscious communication can contradict the verbal cues of conscious communication.

Identifying Unconscious Communication

Remember, unconscious communication is unintentional communication that occurs on a subconscious level. Here are telltale signs of unconscious communication:

1. Repetition

This is where you keep repeating the same verbal statements, communicating underlying nervousness or fear. The more nervous you are, even when you don't physically look like you are, the more likely you are to keep repeating the same phrase over and over.

2. Substitution

This is where you substitute unconscious communication for verbal statements. For example, instead of telling the other person that you are angry with whatever they are saying, you roll your eyes, hiss, and tap your foot like they are wasting your time.

3. Transference

This is where you transfer your emotions or feelings toward something else, deflecting from responding to the issue at hand. For example, you and your friend have had a falling out, and you decide to have a sit down in a restaurant to work through it. The issue at hand has made you very angry with your friend, but instead of talking about the issue that caused the rift and expressing your anger to your friend, you transfer your anger to the server bringing your meal. You yell at them about the cutlery or not being fast enough to bring the breadsticks.

The Impact of Unconscious Communication

Therapists believe that the expressions and gestures that come with unconscious communication are actually our honest signals, and they affect personal and business interactions. We must learn to become aware of our unconscious communication because it impacts what we are "saying" to the world around us.

Let me share the story of World Series Poker champion Phil Hellmuth, who has won the championship eleven times. He wears sunglasses and a hat when playing poker because he wants to disguise his expressions and reactions from other players. Poker is a game of reading the table; even the smallest expression or twitch could tip another player of your hand.

Even after 18 years of playing the game and winning championships, Hellmuth continues to wear a hat and sunglasses.

Most people would think he must be able to control his expression after such a long career. Or keep a poker face. But Hellmuth doesn't take any chances.

According to Dr. Alex Pentland, author of Honest Signals: How They Shape Our World and professor of media, arts, and sciences at MIT, our unconscious, tiny reactions say more than we may want to verbalize, and they don't lie. We can manipulate conscious communication because we know what each word means and how it plays into communication. But some of our actions in unconscious communication betray the real underlying feelings.

For example, you may say that I am happy, but you unconsciously sigh, indicating that you may not be as happy as you want others to believe. Honest signaling happens without us thinking about it, like the sigh. That's what makes it honest and real. Most poker players are still terrible at controlling their back-channel signals.

Unconscious Body Language Communication Signals

In the Legs

The legs are typically a good indicator of what a person is feeling, and they communicate much more than other parts of the body. In unconscious body language, the further the part is from the body, the less control you have over it because it is less possible to fake the "expressions" on extremities.

Some of the ways that legs unconsciously communicate are by:

- Pointing in the direction you want to go when you are ready to leave the room. The foot will unconsciously point toward the door when you decide to leave.

- Subtly moving the genital area, especially when speaking to the opposite sex, shows that you find the other person attractive.

- Taking a wide stance makes the body seem larger to show that you are not afraid and sometimes, to threaten someone. This is a show of dominance. Open legs also show confidence and power.

- Crossed legs show that you are either relaxed or trying to hide something. So depending on the situation, it can be a defensive move or a chilling position. But crossed legs facing away from the person you are communicating with indicate a lack of interest in what they are saying.

- When in the sitting position, open legs indicate relaxation. But crossing your ankles together indicates fear or anxiety while wrapping your legs around yourself indicates shyness or introverted tendencies.

But in some cases, one may need to cross their legs because of their attire (especially women) to avoid exposing themselves.

In the Hands

Hand gestures are the second most expressive form of unconscious communication after the face. Even though hand gestures vary in meaning depending on the various cultures, there are universal hand gestures that convey unconscious communication. They include:

- Holding can be a gentle hold that indicates relaxation or gripping until your knuckles become white, indicating fear, extreme anxiety, or unbearable pain or discomfort. Holding some objects can indicate nervousness because you need something to play with to alleviate the nervousness.

- Hands behind your back, opening up your front, indicating openness to communication or absorption of new ideas.

- Wringing hands can show extreme nervousness.

- Holding yourself in opposite arms indicates self-restraint.

- Crossing your arms indicates being closed off from others.

- Playing with your hands by wringing or picking on an item in front of you indicates nervousness and anxiety.

- Slamming a hand or fist on the table indicates anger, frustration, and even disgust.

- Hands covering the mouth after saying something may mean lying or having said something inappropriate.

- Rubbing your hands can indicate anticipation or being happy about something specific.

- Rapidly tapping your fingers indicates boredom, impatience, or lack of interest.

- Touching yourself may indicate nervousness, while touching others may indicate confidence and trying to make others feel at home around you. The touching could be in terms of grooming where you constantly pat your hair, flick imaginary flint of your clothes or straighten your clothes if you are trying to reinforce yourself as attractive.

- This may also indicate an inferior complex or lack of approval from the other person.

- Trembling hands indicate that you may be afraid or excited. It shows that you have lost control over your limbs, and that's why they have a telltale tremble.

- Hands on the chin indicates pensiveness, while hands on both cheeks may indicate adoration toward the other party in the conversation. Children tend to put both hands on their cheeks when listening to an interesting story or watching an endearing character like the ones on Sesame Street.

In the Face

- A smile can show happiness and contentment

- A grimace shows that you are in pain or discomfort

- A frown indicates anger or frustration, or confusion

- An open mouth indicates surprise

- A sultry look indicates desire

- Raised eyebrows indicate surprise or incredulousness

- A sulky face indicates contempt

- Constant blinking means the person is scared or nervous

- A steady gaze into your eyes as you are having a conversation means that the receiver of the message is interested in what you are saying.

- If a person is biting their lips constantly, it could indicate worry.

- A downturn of the mouth indicates displeasure or tension, while an upward turn indicates relaxation and pleasure.

- Lips pressed together may indicate anger, stress, or anxiety.

- Pinching your nose can indicate fatigue or stress.

A facial expression can tell you whether to trust someone or not. Have you ever heard about seeing a smug look accompanied by an insincere smile and darting eyes making people wary of an individual? Those are telltale signs of a person that you cannot trust the other person because they cannot make eye contact.

In the Entire Body

- Turning your entire body away from the receiver of your message (or the sender) demonstrates a lack of interest in the message.

- Leaning forward when someone is speaking shows interest in their message. The interest can be positive when you accompany it with a smile and negative when you accompany it with a scowl.

- Crossed legs and arms simultaneously indicate being closed off from the message.

- Shrugging indicates that you don't care or are not interested in the message. Sometimes when the receiver of a message doesn't feel like communicating, they may shrug unconsciously, indicating they are not connecting with the message or the message's sender.

- Pacing up and down indicates that the person is impatient or restless.

- Posture also unconsciously communicates to the other person. Sitting with your legs open and arms resting on the sides of the chair indicates openness and welcoming the conversation.

- Sitting far away from the other party indicates hostility, lack of interest, and people who are not comfortable with each other.

The ideal intimate distance between people should be six to eight inches apart. This distance indicates that the people have an intimate relationship that allows them to hug, whisper, or touch.

Personal distance is between loving family members like relatives and close platonic friends. Occasionally these people can veer into the intimate distance, but they are mostly in the personal distance zone. It should be between 1.5 and 4 feet.

Social distance is between people who are formally acquainted with each other, and it is typically between four and 12 feet. This distance communicates friendly interaction as the people get to know each other and interact more often. It can be found in co-workers, schoolmates, and neighbors.

Public distance is reserved for any stranger you meet in public. It is typically between 12 to 25 feet, so it is applicable in a crowd or during a presentation, like a lecture. This also varies from culture to culture, with some cultures being more open to close contact and others prefer distance. For example, many European cultures tend to be open to hugs and kisses on the cheeks, and in Arabic culture, it is acceptable for male relatives and friends to kiss on the cheeks.

But in African cultures, close intimate contact of that nature is reserved for family, and even then, some cultures do not allow male and female relatives to interact in that manner. Handshakes and back slaps are more acceptable among Africans. In the Americas, Latin Americans are more comfortable with close contact, while their North American counterparts prefer distance.

Pro Tip:

Never forget, you do not have to endure uncomfortable body language to communicate effectively. Even people who speak from afar can connect and have a real and deep moment without getting into each other's space. Respecting boundaries is critical for unconscious communication.

Now that we know what to expect from conscious and unconscious communication, it is time to know why you are communicating. Before you begin any communication, you must have a goal for the communication in mind. It may seem obvious, but without this goal, it is easy to lose the plot of the conversation and go down unrelated rabbit holes, then the communication becomes redundant.

Below is a step-by-step guide to understanding your goal in any communication.

To define your goal for communication, you need to ask yourself the following three questions:

1. What did I learn from the data I have gathered (data is what you have heard, read, or thought of)
2. What information from the data would I like the other party to know about or address

3. What would I like to see from this conversation (resolving an issue, understanding each other's points of view, more intimacy, trust, etc.)

Of the three questions, number three is your goal for communication with the other party. Define it with details for yourself, and don't lose sight of it when you have a conversation. Here we give you two scenarios: personal and business, of how you can define your goal in communication.

Personal Scenario

Step One: What did I learn from the data I gathered?

Let's say, for example, you have just been introduced to a new colleague at work and have been becoming better acquainted. And you want to invite them to your place for dinner, but they are from another culture. From the initial interaction, you gather the following data:

- They are from a minority Muslim population under persecution in Bangladesh
- They are engaged to be married
- They have been in your country for a very short time

- Their goal is to settle in your country and start a family here

What did you learn from this data? Your new friend is looking for a community where they can fit in and raise their family. In addition, they are in love, and they may be experiencing some culture shock.

The next phase is to gather data about their culture without asking them direct questions. Asking too many questions at the beginning may come across as an interrogation, and you don't want that. Instead, read about the persecuted Muslim population of Bangladesh to get an idea of what your friend may have been through. Also, do some personal research about what it takes for immigrants to settle in a new country.

Have some intimate information that you can share to make them feel at home and also some things to make life easier for them.

Step Two: What information from the data would I like the other party to know about or address?

In this scenario, you may want your new friend to feel like they have a friend. You may also want to get more information about their upbringing, life and family, and values. That entails asking questions and empathizing with their current situation.

If there is something relatable that you can share with them, like navigating the workplace for success, you can share that information.

Step Three: What would I like to see coming from this conversation?

From this conversation, you want the other person to feel at home and trust you. The goal is to grow your friendship and get to know each other. Also, to help the other person in certain ways, find a community that supports them and accepts them.

Business Scenario

Step One: What did I learn from the data I gathered?

Let's say, for example, that you have the responsibility of evaluating a program at work that deals with gender equality at the workplace. You gather a lot of data on the effectiveness of the program, including:

- The kind of training available in the program

- How do staff members get training in dealing with gender equality?
- The primary weaknesses you identified in this program.

Step Two: What information from the data would I like the other party to know about or address?

You want the recipient of the message to know the scope of the program, what information has been gathered about gender equality at the specific workplace, and any issue arising that requires immediate attention and addressing (as well as those that need long-term solutions).

Step Three: What would I like to see coming from this conversation?

You want this communication to be a catalyst for better implementation of the program. This means the weaknesses identified are resolved, or a plan is developed to resolve them. Finally, you want the recipient of the message to have their own evaluation of the program, so they can know how to implement the next program needed at work.

For example, maybe some of the employees' interviews regarding the program revealed that the employees do not feel that there is gender equality when it comes to promotions. This is excellent data that the company can build on and find solutions that make the workplace better. But its importance can be lost on some executives, so your communication needs to be succinct and clear to show how this affects morale, productivity, and overall cohesion at the workplace.

So the goals of this communication example would be:

- To highlight instances of gender inequality in this workplace
- To show where the weaknesses are in the program
- To offer insights into what the company can do better to improve gender equality

UNDERSTANDING THE OTHER SIDE OF THE COMMUNICATION EQUATION

While we need to be self-aware and goal-oriented in our communication with others, we also have to be understanding of the other side of the communication equation. This means knowing and understanding what affects communication with the other person. So you need to shift the awareness to the other person at some point to facilitate successful communication. Some of the things to be aware of that could affect communication with others include:

Cultural differences

When communication occurs among people of different cultures, it is likely for misunderstanding to occur. That is because the nuances of language, gestures, and communication, in general, are different from place to place.

For example, it is not uncommon in African cultures for women to kneel before their husbands and male relatives when serving them food. This is not practiced in western cultures, and western women may feel offended when they are in the company of such cultures. This may affect how they communicate with the members of such communities. They may show aggression toward the men or consider the women weak for looking "meek."

Or when males interact with Muslim women in some Arab countries, they are not to greet them directly, even with a handshake. This can curtail the natural flow of communication because of traditional and cultural barriers that require a translator to approve the message to the woman. And also, there is no eye contact allowed, or the woman may be considered too forward by the male relatives in her family and deemed to bring dishonor to her family.

Real-life example:

In 2017, major soft drink brand Pepsi had to pull down its ad with Kendall Jenner after it elicited massive backlash because of its message. In the ad, there is a standoff between protestors and police. The ad came at a time of tensions between police and black protestors protesting excessive use of force and police brutality in the United States.

Also, there were calls for diversity in the police force to end racism. The ad features placards calling for love and a cast of diverse cultures and races all joining forces to protest the police. And then Kendall Jenner walks through the midst of the active protesters, grabs a Pepsi as she goes, and sashays to a police officer and offers it to him. The police officer drinks the Pepsi and breaks into a smile. The protesters cheer, hug, and high-five each other, and the protest is forgotten, as are the tensions. All appears to be right in the world again, because of a Pepsi.

The ad failed to communicate the message that Pepsi was trying to convey, which, according to the company statement, was "a global message of unity, peace, and understanding."

Instead, it appeared to make light of the seriousness of protests against police brutality, especially in light of the Black Lives Matter movement and message, which was at the forefront of some protests at the time. The cultural experience of black people in America is tainted by police brutality and protests, which have sometimes been fatal. Having a white model with white privilege merely hand a Pepsi to a policeman to diffuse the tensions of the protest makes a mockery of the actual experience, which revolves around black people being beaten and shot by police in the United States and demanding real and tangible change.

According to Pepsi's CEO, what appeared to be a protest march to most of the audience was actually a peace march. Looking at the Black Lives Matter protest and comparing the images with the Pepsi ad "peace march," many people noticed the same symbols on the placards and the diversity of the people at the protest, which were very similar. That may explain why most people watching the Pepsi ad felt it looked like a Black Lives Matter march.

We all have different cultural experiences, and to communicate well, we must put ourselves in each other's place to empathize and be considerate in how we speak and what we talk about. Even how we present our message must be empathic.

Emotional Intelligence and Maturity

How you speak to others should reflect your under-standing of your emotional intelligence and maturity. For example, you cannot speak to a child the same way you would an adult. The maturity levels deeply affect the way we receive or send messages. That is why children will use tantrums and sulking to get their way instead of articulating their specific needs and convincing their parents to get them what they need.

Children may get away with how they speak because they are not yet mature, but even they grow up and begin to exhibit emotional maturity.

Real-life Example:

Dictators and tyrants tend to have low emotional intelligence, which makes it very hard to communicate with them. Idi Amin is an excellent example of a communicator with low emotional intelligence. He demanded to be addressed using strong terms like "President for Life." That shows he needs to control the conversation or communication by making the other person feel in awe of him. People with high emotional intelligence want to interact and communicate with equals and not with people who feel inferior to them.

Also, such communicators tend to have emotional outbursts, which are synonymous with Idi Amin's rule. He demanded loyalty, and anyone he deemed to fall short of this was branded a traitor to him and the government and was arrested and put to death. This also points to another quality that proves Amin's low emotional intelligence: He lacked empathy.

The inability to feel for other people curtails communication and makes it impossible to connect with others. Dictators like Idi Amin cannot understand the feelings of others or choose to ignore them, so communicating with others becomes an irrelevant burden they don't want to carry.

Previous Experiences

We can carry our previous experiences (good or bad) into our future communication situations. For example, you may expect a bad communication experience with a person of a certain culture based on a history of bad communication with another person of the same culture in another environment.

Or you may expect a great communication experience with someone based on previous conversations with a similar person, only to be disappointed. This could even be the same person who communicates differently at various times.

Real-Life Example:

The rallying call of Winston Churchill made him infamous, and he is touted as one of the greatest communicators of all time. This is despite being bipolar. But those who interacted with him closely saw both sides of his communication, which would make them wary of approaching him sometimes. He would be inspiring and charming at times and then very stubborn and defiant.

This giant of a man was known to be personable during his mild manic phase, but his moods would change quickly, making communication with him a rollercoaster. Sometimes, people didn't know whom they would be dealing with, the charismatic, charming leader or the dark, brooding person he became during his intense manic phases.

Another example is prolific dancer Vaslav Nijinsky, considered the greatest dancer of his time in the early 1900s. He was famous and revered for his ability to take gigantic leaps and dance on his toes, uncommon skills both for male dancers and for overall intense performances. He also had schizophrenia, which caused him to be personable one minute, and other times go for weeks without talking.

Due to this, communication with Nijinsky was unpredictable because you didn't know if the person from the previous experience would be whom you were talking to today, or if there would be complete silence meeting your attempt at conversation.

Misunderstanding the Message

The other person may attach a different meaning to the same word or symbol. For example, you may be speaking to someone and use a curse word that is not offensive to you, but to the other person, it may be very offensive and disrespectful.

Real-life example:

The Hook' Em Horns symbol represents the University of Texas. It is a reference to their mascot, the longhorn, and the symbol references the head and horns of this breed of cattle. Texas is known as the home of longhorn cattle in America.

But in Europe, this symbol is associated with Satanism.

So when former President George W. Bush's daughter Jenna Bush flashed the sign to show her devotion to the University of Texas, Norwegians were appalled.

To them, it seemed like a nod to Satanism, and coming from the first daughter of the United States, whose father is the leader of the free world, it communicated support and maybe even support for the dark religion.

But in this case, the Bushes were merely showing support for their favorite university's marching band as it passed through the inaugural parade in Washington, DC. The Norwegian newspaper *Verdens Gang* had to explain the context to its readers so that they got the right message regarding the use of horns in this context.

Another example is the swastika. Did you know that the swastika used to be an ancient Indian symbol signifying "to be good?" It was even used by an American regiment that had a swastika patch on their uniform during WWI. Some sports teams even used it on their uniforms because it was believed to symbolize good luck. This was before the 20th century, of course – and then Hitler adopted the symbol, and it became associated with Nazism. In Hinduism, the right-facing swastika symbolizes prosperity and good luck, while the left-facing swastika symbolizes tantric aspects of Kali.

So we can understand if some Hindus during WWII may have been confused when Nazi soldiers traveled through their territory wearing swastikas. The swastikas may have communicated that the Nazis were "good," but they actually meant harm and dominance.

Group Affiliations

When we are affiliated with different groups that may be at odds, it can be difficult to communicate with each other. Some affiliations are by choice, while others are because of where we grew up or family ties.

Real-life example:

The Ku Klux Klan remains one of the most hateful and racist groups in the United States that has fueled hate for black people and other minorities. Their hateful rhetoric and beliefs make it hard to communicate with others, even Caucasians who don't hold the same beliefs.

For example, communication between the Klan and black Americans is typically nonexistent because of the insulting terms and tone the Klan holds when addressing Africans, not to mention the lynching and killings. And communication with the contemporary white power movement is also hampered because the Klan insists on holding on to unpopular imagery and rituals to assert their supremacy.

Communication between the Klan and other groups is bound to be hostile and ineffective.

Education Level

The recipient of your message may not have the same level of education as you, which hampers their ability to understand your message.

Real-life Example:

In the medical world, there is a lot of jargon that the patient does not understand because of their education level. Doctors have gone to school for years to learn how to diagnose and treat our diseases, so when they explain our ailments, we may not understand because our levels of education are not at par.

Communication barriers due to a difference in educational levels occur daily.

There is also a difference in intellectual levels. You cannot treat a toddler as your intellectual equal, so communicating with them with adult intellectual maturity could be lost on them.

UNDERSTANDING THE SITUATION

Once you understand both sides of the communication equation, it is time to understand the situation correctly. Communication can be staged or impromptu. Understand the right situation to have an impromptu communication and which situation calls for staging an appropriate area for the conversation to take place.

Staged communication is where we choose the location or setting for the conversation, send emails concerning what we are talking about, and have experts around to offer their expertise on the subject matter. Sometimes, we can stage a conversation between friends by choosing the location and setting and knowing what we will discuss.

Impromptu communication is an unscheduled meeting where conversations occur naturally. Typically impromptu communication is not used to resolve any existing issues; instead, we get to know how the other person has been since we last saw each other.

When it comes to staged communication, there are three aspects to consider:

The location: Choose a location that allows you to communicate freely and without distractions and other hindrances.

For example, a packed restaurant may not be the best place to have a conversation resolving an existing issue between two people. You may be unable to hear each other over other diners' conversations. Also, you may be unable to express yourself freely for fear of others overhearing your conversation, especially if it is private.

The timing: Do not begin a conversation when they are in the middle of another one or when they have a work deadline. Instead, get in touch with the other person and schedule some time when you are both free and able to speak. That shows that you respect their time, and the ensuing conversation between you two is important.

The person: Do not have the right conversation with the wrong person. For example, you may want a raise at work, but instead of talking to the boss, you talk to colleagues, family, and friends who, unfortunately, cannot give you the raise even when they feel you deserve it. Have a conversation with the right person. Sometimes going around telling everyone you want a raise may offend the boss when they get wind of what you are saying without hearing it directly from you.

3

DON'T JUST HEAR PEOPLE

To hear people, you have to listen. Listening is critical in communication because it informs you how to respond to the communication.

> *"Listening is not just hearing what someone tells you word for word. You have to listen with a heart. I don't want that to sound touchy-feely; it is not. It is very hard work."*
>
> — ANNA DEAVERE SMITH

People who just hear others engage in what we call passive listening. Passive listening is when we do not respond or provide feedback and sometimes don't even understand the message. It is one-way communication.

But people who listen practice active listening, which means they respond with a smile, nod, or raised eyebrows. This tells the other party in the conversation that we understand what they are saying and can relate to their experience.

Practicing active listening allows you to do more than hear people; it helps you connect.

Here are the requirements of good listening:

ALLOW OTHERS TO FINISH THEIR STATEMENTS

It is common courtesy to allow the other person to complete what they are saying before you respond. When we jump into what the other person is saying before they complete their sentence, it clearly indicates that we are not really listening. Instead, we just want to communicate our points regardless of the other person's feelings or point of view.

Talk shows are guilty of this behavior, especially political shows. The louder you are, and the more you hammer your point across, the more you believe you are making your point. The quieter people are drowned in the melee and end up not getting heard. In everyday life, no one wants to talk to someone who doesn't listen and instead talks over them and repeats the same talking points over and over.

There are several things that your interruption says to the other person:

a) I don't care what you have to say

b) My voice, opinion, point of view, or information is the only important thing in this conversation

c) I don't have the patience to sit through this communication process

What to Do?

If someone interrupts you when you are speaking, here are a few expressions you can use to regain control of the conversation:

- We are definitely talking about that next, but right now...

- Sure thing, but I don't want us to forget this point about...

- I am curious about that too but let's get back to it in a minute...

- That is a great point you have there; let's return to that after...

These are polite ways to respond to an interruption and continue your conversation without putting the other person on the spot.

ASK QUESTIONS TO SEEK CLARIFICATION

A good listener never assumes anything. If a point is unclear, it is vital to seek clarification to understand the message clearly. Also, asking questions indicates that you are interested in what the other person is saying, and you want to go deeper into the substance of what they are talking about.

What to Do?

- Doing this requires you to ask in-depth follow-up questions and ask for the other party to articulate their points clearly.

- Begin by asking the original question again but soften your tone so that you do not sound adversarial.

- Ask if there is anything the other party would like to say about the matter.

- Ask if you have understood the message correctly.

MAINTAIN ACTIVE LISTENING BODY LANGUAGE

There are things that you can do to encourage the other party to continue talking to you. Maintaining body language that helps others feel free to talk to you is essential. Body language changes the context of our communication completely. When we sit rigidly while listening, the other person is not inspired to talk to us, no matter how animated they may be.

But when an equally enthusiastic listener reciprocates an animated speaker's communication, communication becomes a beautiful dance.

What to Do?

- Hold a steady but warm gaze with the speaker as they speak

- Lean forward where appropriate to show a keen interest

- Smile where appropriate

- Nod where appropriate

- Place your hands with the palms facing upward

- Incline your head toward the person speaking

PROVIDE FEEDBACK

Feedback is a critical part of communication, so be open to giving the other party feedback when asked. Some speakers do not want feedback, so do not force it on them. Instead, you can paraphrase their points with respect to reinforcing their ideas, or allow them to hear their ideas repeated back to them to see if they are sound.

What to Do?

- Make sure the feedback is constructive

- Ensure the feedback is based on the message shared by the other person

- Only offer feedback when it is asked for

- It is better to have one-on-one conversations during feedback, where the other party may receive the message with any nuance intended, rather than giving written feedback, which has a greater potential for misunderstanding.

HAVE OPEN BODY LANGUAGE

Non-verbal cues are essential to listening. Have open body language that allows others to see you as approachable. This is vital for the other person to feel comfortable talking to you. It shows them that you are open to having a detailed conversation, and they can benefit from communication with you.

What to Do?

- Do not cross your arms or legs; keep your body open.

- Listen intently with bright eyes, avoid brooding eyes or looking at the other party through slit eyes

- If possible, do not have furniture between you like a table. Some of the most successful and reputable political talk show hosts use this technique to interview presidents, prime ministers, and other high-value people.

BEYOND LISTENING

Listening beyond hearing is described as being very engaged in the communication process. Many experts believe that listening beyond hearing engages our hearts, intuition, and senses. When we engage in listening beyond hearing, we do the following:

Strengthen our sense-abilities

The sensory abilities include hearing, seeing, smell, touch, and taste. Using our senses, we can see expressions and hear words that determine the direction of the communication process. In communication, it is critical to use our senses in the communication process.

Focus on hearing the words, on looking at the facial expressions and the body language. In some cultures, bitter food is served when having difficult conversations so that those engaging in the conversation are reminded of the challenge. For example, the Passover feast and the festival of unleavened bread is a reminder of a terrible time in Jewish history. The taste of the food is meant to communicate the harsh and bitter reality of this historical time of slavery and the cost of deliverance.

And touch can communicate aggression or care. If you are speaking with someone and they slap you or grab you hard, your sense of touch tells you that there is aggression in the other party, while a friendly pat or gentle touch can calm you down and even endear you to the other person.

Listen from a holistic perspective

Holistic listening is listening to the entire text, allowing you to hear all the details the other person is happy to share. On the flip side, there is segment listening, where you listen to certain aspects of the conversation that fit into the direction you want the communication to take.

The holistic perspective to communication is to speak with more than just the voice. So the holistic listening perspective allows you to hear the entirety of the conversation while also listening for cues to follow up on that the other party emphasizes.

Nurture relationships

To nurture relationships, we have to learn to listen beyond hearing, allowing the communication flow to be flawless. After all, you have an easy communication flow with people you have a relationship with compared to strangers to you.

To nurture a relationship, you must spend time together, speak honestly, and be open. But also great relationships that are worth nurturing tend to be with quality connections, and listening beyond hearing is crucial to nurturing any relationship you value.

When you learn to listen beyond hearing over time, you have the following outcomes:

1. Value-based relationships with high-quality connections

2. Strengthening and practicing holistic communication
3. Suspension of assumptions and judgement so that you can understand the point of view of other people
4. Be fully present in all communications you engage in

WATCH YOUR LANGUAGE

Language is essential in communication, and our words are not only powerful but also damaging or building, depending on how we use them. To use language properly, we have to define it and assign its function to our lives. This allows us to understand how to use language and what types of words could cause miscommunication.

WHAT IS LANGUAGE?

According to the dictionary, language is the primary method humans use to communicate with each other in a particular country or community. It comprises words, grammatical structure, and vocabulary that are all conveyed in speech.

But in the context of effective communication, the quote below conveys language best:

> *"Our language is the reflection of ourselves. A language is an exact reflection of the character and growth of its speakers."*
>
> — CESAR CHAVEZ

I have broken down the definition of language into three areas that apply to us daily.

1. It is a grouping of words and expressions that are understood and used by a large group of people
2. It is symbols and sounds that are written or spoken by a particular group of people
3. It is an expression of ideas and feelings in sign language

That means that language is spoken, written, or signaled.

THE FUNCTION OF LANGUAGE

Without language, we cannot communicate effectively with each other. That is why people who speak different languages have difficulty communicating and understanding each other. Bible readers may have come across the story of the tower of Babel. It is one of the best examples of what happens when we cannot speak the same language. Christians believe this was the origin of the diversity of languages.

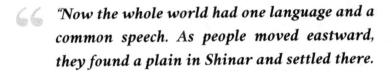

"Now the whole world had one language and a common speech. As people moved eastward, they found a plain in Shinar and settled there.

They said to each other, "Come let us make bricks and bake them thoroughly." They used the bricks instead of stone and tar instead of mortar. Then they said, "Come, let us build ourselves a city, with a tower that reaches to the heavens so that we may make a name for ourselves; otherwise, we will be scattered all over the face of the whole earth."

But the Lord came down to see the city and the tower the people were building. The Lord said, "If as one people, speaking the same language they have begun to do this, then nothing they plan to do will be impossible for them. Come, let us go down and confuse their language so they will not understand each other."

— **GENESIS 11: 1-9**

According to this Bible story, God confused the language of the whole world, which scattered them all over the earth according to their new languages.

But then we have other scientific records that date language back two million years ago and roughly 150,000 years ago.

Whichever version of the origin of language you believe in, we can all agree that the function of language was to bring us together in our specific groupings for the following purposes:

- Communication
- Expression
- Identity
- Emotional release
- Play
- Imaginative creativity

Communication:

Communication in language is the interactional function. It allows you to exchange words and expressions, resulting in interaction and conversation. As an interactional function, it enables you to form and develop social relationships and eases interactions. For example, when we use slang to communicate, we connect on a social level.

Expression:

Expression in language is the regulatory function. That means it is used to influence and regulate the behavior of others by letting them know how you feel. For example, when you express dissatisfaction with another person, they regulate their behavior, so they can remedy the situation and restore balance to your relationship. In this way, your language has influenced and regulated theirs.

Identity:

Identity in language is the personal function. In this regard, language allows you to express your opinions, preferences, and personality, all of which make up your identity. This allows people that you communicate with to get to know you better. For example, African Americans have a certain flow of words in how they speak, which is part of their identity. Here are some words that are part of the African American language that contribute to their identity:

- Bling – Flashy jewelry that creates an impression of wealth
- Hang – To hang out with friends or family
- Chill out - To take it easy
- Bomb or da bomb – something is extremely nice
- Diss – To talk disparagingly to someone or insult them
- Dope – Something is awesome
- Snatched – Someone looks great
- Lit – Something is exciting or amazing
- Sick – Something is very cool
- Thick - A curvy woman
- Gucci – Everything is good or going well

Emotional release:

Emotional release in language is the representational function. That means it is used to exchange ideas and also express emotion. For example, the spoken word uses poetic and flowery language to offer the emotional release of how the performer is feeling about their environment. Certain metaphors represent the performer's emotional state and relay their message better than an ordinary conversation would.

Play:

Play in language is the heuristic function. That means it allows us to explore our environment, especially for children who are still learning new words and how to express themselves in their environment. A child utilizes words and expressions to learn through questions, answers, and monologues. Do you notice that a running commentary usually accompanies children at play even when they do not have someone they are talking to? That is the heuristic function at work.

Imaginative creativity:

Imaginative creativity in language is the imaginative function. This aspect of language allows us to explore our imaginations and create ideas and storylines that feed into our fantasies. Imaginative creativity enables us to tell stories that capture the imagination of our audiences, tell a joke so well it leaves others breathless with laughter, or relate a story so compellingly that we emotionally make others around us. This is where dramas, music, films, poetry, and the arts come from.

ELEMENTS OF LANGUAGE

There are five fundamental elements of language that guide how we communicate. Understanding these elements of language allows us to be fluid in communication regardless of what setting we find ourselves in.

Element #1: Language is Communicative

This means that language conveys messages and dispenses information. That is why language is passed down from generation to generation because it passes information, traditions, and cultural norms to those who come after us. All civilizations had a way of preserving the language, particularly in writing, to instruct the younger generations and sustain their society. Without practicing a language, we will lose it, and that is why we are taught vocabulary and grammar. Existing ancient texts tell us how people lived centuries ago because we can understand the language in the texts.

Element #2: Language has Structure

There is no language in the world that doesn't have structure. The structure is found in the organized pattern of the language that gives it shape. Typically, this structure tends to be familiar to all users of that language so they can all understand each other. The building blocks that form the pattern of a language include:

- Phonology (the sounds)
- Lexicon (the vocabulary)
- Morphology (The grammar)
- Syntax (the rules that determine the order of elements in a sentence)
- Semantics (interpretation of meanings)

These are the blueprint of how our languages work and make language intelligible to all of us.

Element #3: Language is Arbitrary

Even with the structure we must follow for language to make sense, language remains arbitrary. As such, language doesn't have to be constant in all countries and communities. For example, in English we say "no," but the same word in German is "niet," in Swahili it is "hapana," and it is "nahin" in Hindi. Does the word cease to mean the same thing, just because it is said differently in various languages? No—it remains the same word.

These words exist as part of a system, and the specific culture determines that system. That allows words not to be predictable.

Element #4: Language Embraces Dynamism

Language is not a rigid entity because it is perpetually morphing and evolving, giving it a life of its own. That is why the dictionary is constantly being updated with new English words. Twenty years ago, words like adulting, awe-walking, sapiosexual, and whataboutism did not exist in the dictionary. They were added in 2021 to keep up with the ever-evolving and fluidness of our language in this age.

I love to travel and have frequented many countries as a result. One of my favorite countries to visit is Kenya. And during my travels, I picked up on their slang, which is a mixture of the official language of English, the national language of Swahili, and the various languages spoken in the country. The slang is known as "Sheng." The first time I went, I was in the central business district, and my guide asked a guard if there was any rioting, since a protest had been planned for the day. The guard informed him that the government banned the protest, hence the heavy police presence in the CBD.

And my guard said, "**kun'gam diambo mapema ni muhimu.**"

This means knowing about any trouble in advance is important.

I recently visited Kenya and hired the same guide. Years on, he told me that the sheng has changed so much that he has to learn new words to keep up with the current generation's use of the language. I asked him about the above phrase and what it sounds like now. Here is what it sounds like now:

"**Kukemba ngori ni muhimu.**"

The two phrases mean the same thing, but they show the evolution of the language.

Another example is when they say: Ninaenda mboka, which means I am going to work. Mboka is derived from the Swahili word mboga, which are vegetables eaten at meal times. So saying "ninaenda mboka" means I am going to work for my daily meal (mboga).

This happens in all languages, as all languages are fluid and change.

Element #5: Language Generates and is Renewable

Languages allow us to communicate the same thing with new catchphrases and structures. This keeps language alive and generative. For example, Latin is considered an old dead language, as is Old English. But people who practice Latin still keep it alive by speaking it. However, old English died after generating new English because no one practiced it anymore. We can keep a language alive by practicing it like Latin is used in Vatican City and is recognized as one of its official languages. But in the case of Old English, no one ever walks around saying, "Whole be thou" for hello and "God be with ye" for goodbye.

THE PLACE OF JARGON IN LANGUAGE

Jargon is not a separate language element but another part of language that specific groups use due to their shared interest. For example, all doctors worldwide tend to use the same medical argon because of their shared work experience. As a result, jargon breaks down the complex ideas of a specific industry into a language that is summarized and easy to understand for that specific target group. For example, medical jargon may be complex to the layperson, but it is understandable to medical doctors.

Some experts believe jargon complicates language unnecessarily, while others believe it is necessary for specific industries. So here are some rules to consider if you have to use technical language (jargon):

- Use jargon only with an audience that understands it. So do not apply jargon to a conversation or writing meant for a general audience. For example, when communicating with fellow doctors, saying the patient was suffering from laryngitis is okay. But for a general audience, it is better to say the patient had a sore throat.

- Avoid using technical terms without explanation. Mention it the first time and explain it so that the next time you use it, the audience will know what it means.

- Do not repeat the same jargon in every sentence. That doesn't make you sound informed or educated but rather rigid and not creative. Jargon tends to limit communication flow, making it harder for others to connect with you.

- If you are using new industry jargon, ensure that you explain it even if you are talking to people who are in the industry like you. Remember, jargon is also ever-evolving, and new acronyms and jargon are introduced all the time: Not everyone can keep up. So if you use it, explain it.

- Present jargon in your own unique way to keep the language smooth and flowing. Many people who use jargon use it stiffly, so the communication is boring and dry. This causes them to come across as people who do not know the meaning of the jargon they are using or trying too hard to sound smart.

LANGUAGE STYLES

We all use different language styles at one point or another in our communication with others. Language style refers to the form of language we choose to communicate formally or informally. These forms of language include:

1) *Verbal Language Styles:*

- Oratorical (also known as frozen) style
- Formal style
- Casual style
- Consultative style
- Intimate style

The Oratorical Style

There are two approaches to the oratorical language style, and both tend to be long and winding formal speeches.

The first approach is communication for people who are strangers. It does not require participation and the tone tends to be monotone. It is adapted for presentations by students in a class presentation or employees presenting a project at work. Since the recipient of the message is socially strange to the sender, the latter doesn't feel the need to connect with the former. Also, the message may not be compelling enough to make the sender feel passionate about it.

The second approach is a more passionate and compelling message shared by a motivated sender and enthusiastic recipient. This can be a campaign speech or a toast. In this case, the speech can be puffy and self-important or down-to-earth and relatable. President Obama is well known and respected for his down-to-earth yet very compelling campaign speeches.

The word oratorical is derived from the Latin word oratorius, which means "pleading or speaking." In fact, this language style is believed to leave the recipient pleading to the speaker to either stop or continue.

Examples of oratorical language style:

- Class presentations
- Work presentations
- Eulogies
- Wedding toast

- Retirement toast

The Formal Style

This language style features a formal, professional tone that leaves no room for slang. Formal language can be quite rigid, leaving the speaker to focus on being deliberate in their message delivery. The message has to be formulated in advance for the formal aspect of the conversation to be felt. Usually, the speaker has written the message, and they do not deviate from it regardless of the setting.

Examples of formal language style:

- Presidential speeches
- Speeches by company executives

The Casual Style

Friends and close acquaintances use this language style, but it can also be used on someone who is being accepted as a new member of a circle of friends. The casual language style allows the use of first names and nicknames you create for each other. Also, there is the use of slang, and no one pays attention to the proper sentences and grammar.

Examples of casual language style:

- Between members of a club
- Among teenagers and college students

The Consultative Style

This language style allows the recipient and the sender to draw from each other's experiences and expertise. It is collaborative, which makes it mutually respectful for the speaker and the listener. That is why it has a formal approach but the freedom to use flamboyant language to impress each other.

Examples of consultative language style:

- During lectures
- During brainstorming meetings

The Intimate Style

This language style is used between people in intimate relationships, like sexual partners, married couples, and people courting. The information exchanged is sensitive, so the language is not formal, but it is clear and endearing. Words of affection tend to pepper this language style building the bond of intimacy. There is no need for words that impress; instead, words that inspire trust are more common.

Examples of intimate language style:

- During a date
- During an intimate exchange

2) Written Language Styles

We use four main types of writing language styles daily in our communication. They are:

- Persuasive style
- Expository style
- Narrative style
- Descriptive style

The Persuasive Style

In this style, the writer tries to convince the recipient of the message to accept a certain argument or position in agreement with the sender. So this kind of language has many of the writer's opinions and justification based on their thinking.

Examples of persuasive language style:

- Opinion pieces in the newspaper
- Editorial pieces in the newspaper
- Letter of recommendation

- Argumentative essays in academic papers

The Expository Style

This language style in writing is used to explain a concept or point of view. The writer shares their data, statistics, and evidence to support certain facts with the aim of sharing the same information with their audience. The expository language is not meant to express the writer's opinions but only to share information.

Examples of expository language style:

- Textbooks
- Scientific writing
- How-to articles
- News articles (but not Op-Eds or editorials)
- Business writing

The Narrative Style

This written language style is seen in longer writing samples. The narrative style shares information within a story, and it features the main characters and a setting where the action takes place.

Examples of narrative language style:

- Novels
- Biographies
- Historical accounts

The Descriptive Style

This language style depicts imagery using words to imprint a clear picture in the reader's mind. The reader becomes more connected to the story as they create the visuals in their brain and use their senses to bring the visuals to life. In descriptive, we use metaphors, similes, and other descriptive techniques to connect and engage with the audience.

Examples of descriptive language style:

- Poetry
- Memoirs
- First-hand accounts of events
- Fictional novels

THE DIFFERENCE BETWEEN ORAL AND WRITTEN LANGUAGE

- Oral language is more personal
- Oral language is repetitive

- Oral language is less formal

Oral language is less formal and has a more direct feel as you look at the other person directly in the eyes when speaking. It can also be more repetitive without looking awkward, as it would in written form. That is because written language relies on a larger vocabulary than oral language.

You also have the opportunity to use gestures and facial expressions in oral language as the other person can see your face and body language and read them as well. The speech also allows you to use tone to support your words, making communication easier to decipher.

APPROPRIATE LANGUAGE

Appropriate language is language that we can use in all settings without making others in the same environment uncomfortable. The language is fitting for the audience and context. Imagine if President Barack Obama used curse words when talking to his base during his campaigns. Not only would he appear unsuited for the office he was seeking, since the position entails speaking with foreign dignitaries, but he would also come across as disrespectful to his audience.

That doesn't mean that his language needs to be bland and boring. In fact, President Obama used his language skills expertly to engage the crowd in a very oratory and formal language format, without using the typical approach of the regular language styles.

So what makes appropriate language?

- Choosing words that accurately reflect your feelings, ideas, and thought on the subject matter

- Avoid using slang that alienates other people who are not of your culture or community

- Avoid using profanity since that could be offensive to your audience

- Only use words that you know the meaning of

- Avoid making blanket statements that blame one segment of your audience

- Always ensure that your audience understands you by asking if you are understood

- Use simple language that everyone can understand

Appropriate language in business

Standard English is an acceptable and appropriate language in business and the workplace. Some people of the same culture may find it easy to communicate in their native language. Still, in the workplace or business, that can be discriminatory as it shuts out other team members.

It is best to maintain a formal approach to language at work or in business to keep interactions professional and respectful.

Appropriate language in the home

Children and minors learn from example and hearing. So if you use derogatory or abusive language around them, they regurgitate the same language in their interactions with other kids. Use respectful language at home to show all family members you respect them.

Respect begins at home for both adults and children, so address each other with respectful and endearing words that build each other up.

Appropriate language in public

Do not use derogatory language to describe people of different ethnicities or cultures. Also, avoid making stereotypical statements because they use offensive language. They are meant to put the other person down and dehumanize them. Some people hide behind jokes, but even jokes can be inappropriate because they use derogatory language.

In some cases, even when talking to members of the same culture and community, avoid derogatory slang that is inappropriate for others to hear. Instead, strive to be polite and kind. The lessons we learned as children about saying *please, excuse me,* and *thank you* apply today and should be language passed down through generations.

Pro Tip:

If you are struggling with identifying what is appropriate language, there are great online classes that teach the principles of language to follow.

One of the major issues we grapple with may not be inappropriate language but rather unsupportive language. You may not use profanity, but you say things that break the other person.

For example, you tell your significant other that you wouldn't trust them to make a sound financial decision. You may not have called them stupid outright, but your language has implied that they cannot make useful or healthy financial decisions. It means they are diminished in your sight, and this can be considered an insult to their financial intelligence.

TYPES OF UNSUPPORTIVE LANGUAGE

Sarcasm:

Sarcasm uses mockery to convey a message of contempt. The chosen words are meant to cut or sting the other person. It intentionally inflicts pain by ridiculing, taunting, or deriding the other person. Many people tend to hide behind such language calling it sharp wit, but it is cutting words meant to make the other person feel small.

Labeling:

Labeling language is meant to put others in a box and shame them into feeling inferior, either due to their history or decisions. You rely on information about the other person to label them negatively, which diminishes their abilities and capabilities.

Judgmental messages:

This is passing judgement on another person based on the very limited information that you may have. For example, you may refuse an employee a raise because they were late a few times, and you quickly judge them for their late coming without knowing the reason why.

Maybe they have a long commute, no car to get to work, or a child to care for before heading to work.

In a meeting, you may single them out with phrases like "here comes the perpetual latecomer," which influences other employees, causing them to look at this particular employee in poor judgement. They may treat this employee poorly because of your judgmental message.

Threats:

Threats are unsupportive messages that make the other person feel unsafe and unwanted. To use threats means to use insulting and aggressive language, which tells the other person that you do not have their best interests at heart and don't care about their wellbeing.

Negative comparisons:

You do not typically use supportive language when you compare people negatively to others. For example, you tell your child, "Look at the smart decisions your sister makes, and why can't you be more like her?" You are breaking down the child's sense of self-confidence and worth, so they feel like just being themselves is not enough; they have to be like someone else to be enough.

5

BODIES COMMUNICATE

The role of the body in communication comes down to the use of facial expressions, gestures, and body placement to communicate a message. This is called non-verbal communication, which speaks even louder than what you say. People look more at your body language than what you are saying. That is why the phrase "giving lip service" exists. This means that you are just saying the right things, but your body is saying something entirely different.

Your mannerisms, physical behavior, and expressions, which are often instinctive, say more than what your words may be saying. For example, you may say, "I am fine," but you have a frown on your face, and your hands are balled into fists. Even silence communicates a message non-verbally.

Non-verbal communication is extremely important because it:

- **Reinforces the real message you are communicating**

If your verbal message is the same as your non-verbal message, the non-verbal cues reinforce your message. In fact, the non-verbal cues unconsciously repeat the message.

- **Contradicts the false verbal message**

If your verbal message is false, the non-verbal cues communicate the real message and repeat it repetitively, so the other person knows your real message. This indicates to the other person that you are not telling them the truth.

- **Complements the initial message**

Non-verbal cues complement the initial message. For example, if you are praising someone and patting them on the back, the pat, which is a non-verbal cue, complements your verbal message.

- **Substitutes the verbal message**

Sometimes you may not be able to express yourself verbally due to being overly emotional or scared. The non-verbal cues act as a substitute for the lack of words. For example, tears can convey grief more than words ever can.

- **Accentuates the verbal message**

In some cases, you need non-verbal cues to accentuate your verbal message. For example, you may want to convey how upset you are, so in addition to letting the other person know your feelings verbally, you also pound the table to emphasize your displeasure.

HOW TO READ BODY LANGUAGE

There are many telltale signs that you can pick up from a person's body language to clue you in on what the other person is really feeling. Here is how you can read body language:

Look at the Gestures

There are four types of hand gestures in body language. They are:

- Beat gestures
- Iconic gestures
- Deictic gestures
- Metaphoric gestures

Beat Gestures

Beat gestures are the most commonly used gestures that accompany speech. They are spontaneously produced hand movements that are in tune with the rhythm of the speech. Interestingly these gestures are used regardless of whether you can see the person you are talking to or not.

Examples of beat gestures:

- Up and down movements that coincide with the end of a sentence
- Back and forth movements occurring during speech
- Gently pounding the table as you make a point

Iconic Gestures

Iconic gestures represent the meaning or are closely related to the semantic content of the words or speech. They tend to display the physical properties of the objects or actions they accompany during speech.

These manual gestures can describe an action even better than words only.

Examples of iconic gestures:

- Holding up the thumb and forefinger close to each other, meaning that something is small.

Deictic Gestures

These gestures are used to single out an object or person during speech. All pointing gestures are deictic gestures even when you do not use your index finger directly. Deictic gestures occur across all cultures, and in children, they are used to determine whether an infant is aware of what other people pay attention to. These gestures direct the recipient's attention to a specific object or situation in their environment.

Examples of deictic gestures:

- When children point at an object of interest using their index finger.
- During the weather forecast, when the weather person shows the movement of a hurricane or storm.

Metaphoric Gestures

These gestures create a physical representation of an abstract concept to give it more semantic meaning. They tend to be related to a person's mental state, thoughts, and feelings. Using metaphoric gestures gives life to the quirks of thought and feeling as you speak.

Examples of metaphoric gestures:

- Framing your hands into the heart shape and placing them on your chest to indicate to the other person that you love them
- Holding up a fist in the air to show solidarity

Be Aware of Proximity

Proximity shows others whether our communication is aggressive or non-aggressive. Close proximity to a stranger can be read as intent to be aggressive, but the same proximity to a friend is welcome and even encouraged. All cultures have their own approach to proximity, which informs our actions as we grow up.

In the second chapter, we have described four distances we adhere to depending on whom we are talking to. They are

1. Intimate distance (6-8 inches apart)
2. Personal distance (1.5 – four feet)
3. Social distance (4 -12 feet)
4. Public distance (12 – 25 feet)

These distances are used depending on the relationship between the people communicating. But these distances are considered the standard in western cultures. Other cultures may have different rules when it comes to distance.

Also, these distances may not be easy to effect if you have to use public transport, which tends to be over-crowded in most parts of the world. During rush hour, even total strangers have to be in close proximity to each other due to the number of people using the public transport system. However, that doesn't mean that people are now intimate because they are crammed into the carriages on the trains. In fact, most people do not make eye contact, and their bodies are rigid or tense despite their close proximity.

Study the Eyes

The eyes are the mirror of the soul and our minds and are placed in the strongest focal point on the face. The reason why eyes are considered mirrors is that you cannot artificially manipulate the pupils to lie in response to stimuli. They dilate and contract depending on the emotion we are feeling.

Establishing eye contact with the other person allows you to see the response to your words as their pupils tell more about the underlying emotions than words ever could. When the person is happy or excited, their pupils dilate up to four times their usual size, and when angry or aggressive, they contract, creating what is known as "beady or snake eyes." The lighter the eyes, the easier it is to notice the contraction and dilation.

Study the Face

Many things are happening on the face as we communicate, so studying the face can give insight into the real emotions of the person you are talking to. Some people raise an eyebrow unconsciously when they don't believe what you are saying, while others purse their lips when thinking about your words. Other people look at you from under their lashes, as Princess Diana was known to do, and others look down at you over the bridge of their noses.

Most facial expressions slip out unconsciously, indicating the real feelings of the person you are communicating with. So look out for the subtle movement of the mouth, tightening of facial muscles, a suppressed telltale smile, a fleeting frown that came and went too quickly, or a smoothening of the brow, among others.

Watch the Head Movement

Sometimes we do not pay attention to the head movement because we expect the head to move from side to side as someone talks. But there is a lot of communication emanating from head movements that can be subtle. The obvious head movement is nodding and shaking the head. Here are some of the head body language movements to be aware of:

- Holding the head up: It means I am confident and proud of myself

- Head nod up: It means the person is self-assured

- Head nod down: It indicates humility and respect (common in Asian cultures)

- Nodding up and down: This indicates agreement in men, and in women, it indicates both empathy and agreement. It could also be encouraging the speaker to continue talking. Hurried nodding indicates that you are in a hurry for the other person to finish talking so you can say your piece.

- Playing with the hair: This shows you are comfortable in your own skin. It is also the same with the hair toss and flick.

- Gentle touch: This is a reassuring touch.

- Ruffling the hair: This shows that the person is not comfortable

- Rubbing the neck: This also shows you are uncomfortable or apprehensive

- Darting eyes: This indicates fear

- Holding your temples with both hands: This indicates that you are trying to protect yourself, and it also indicates astonishment, like you are wondering what happened.

- Rubbing the forehead: It means someone is dumbfounded, trying to understand, or confused.

- Hanging your head down: This typically means you do not want eye contact either because of fear, anxiety, or shame

- Turning the head away: This means you are not interested in what the other person is saying. Or it could mean you disagree with them.

- Hands on the head: This indicates feeling overwhelmed, frustrated, or stressed.

- The double take: This is when a person looks at you, turns away, and looks again. It indicates incredulity or disbelief. Typically someone is thinking, "Did you just say that?"

- The forehead slap: This also indicates that the other person doesn't believe what you just said. It can also be used when we realize we have just made a silly, obvious mistake.

- Eye rolling: This indicates that you are annoyed by what the other person is saying.

- Head leaning on hand: This movement indicates sadness or the feeling of despair. It may also mean that you are thinking deeply about something that is disturbing your peace. But sometimes, a friend may lean their head on their hand to listen deeply to something interesting you are saying or to pay attention.

- Removing your hat: It indicates respect for the other person or environment. But if you snatch the hat off your head, it could indicate frustration or anger.

Cultural anomalies in head body language

- The head wobble: This is a cultural thing, especially for Indians, which is their equivalent of nodding, agreement, or understanding.

- Yes and no exchange: In Bulgaria, Turkey, Greece, Bengal, and Iran, the nod is actually saying no and not yes, as it is in other cultures.

Pay Attention to Arm Positioning

Arms convey a message as well, when you are looking at body language. They offer a subtler message compared to the apparent head movements mentioned above.

A man positioning his arms, so his hands cover the genitals indicates protective body language. This may indicate that the man feels threatened and they are ready to protect themselves against the threat. Crossing your arms indicates closed body language, meaning you are not open to hearing or agreeing with what the other person is saying. Crossing your arms over your chest, and then leaning back into the chair while looking at the other person over the bridge of your nose, could indicate a challenge or dare. If you stay in this position for long, you will notice the other person losing interest in talking to you or becoming aggravated when communicating with you.

Arm gripping indicates fear or anxiety and also insecurity. On the other hand, crossed arms with hands tucked into the armpit and thumbs pointing upward indicate attentiveness when two people are talking.

Half-hugs where the other person envelops you with their arm indicate filial love and affection. But if the hug is limp and the arm is quickly taken away immediately after, it indicates that the other person is not comfortable around you. Women tend to prefer this hug in order not to feel too exposed by the full-frontal hug.

When the arms cross in the front and rest on the abdomen, this body language indicates one is trying to feel confident. You may notice that game show participants take this stance frequently as they try to answer the questions correctly. Unconsciously they are mentally protecting themselves from a "full frontal attack" as the questions come at them from the person standing right in front of them. It is the same stance when people are standing in the queue to receive money or welfare because they are unconsciously mentally protecting their vulnerable and fragile state of mind and emotions. It is commonly referred to as the fig leaf position. Interestingly, Adolf Hitler adopted this stance to protect himself from feeling inadequate due to having only one testicle.

Look at the Feet

When someone is interested in what you are saying, they sit with their feet facing you and firmly planted on the ground. This means the person is attracted to you and interested in being around you. If someone is happy, their feet could be dancing under the table or twitching up and down lazily.

But if they are anxious, their feet could be apart yet turned inwards to face each other. Some people's feet tap rapidly to indicate that they are anxious. Disinterested people have their feet facing away from you because they are not interested in what you are saying. The feet could be facing toward the door as the person looks for an exit strategy.

When approaching someone and their feet form a V shape, they are interested in what you are saying and look forward to interacting with you. A woman on a date with her shoe dangling off her foot is feeling flirtatious and playful. And if someone has one foot ahead of the other while facing you, it indicates that they are attracted to you and interested in what you are saying. In fact, this is a non-verbal way of saying, "I am very interested in you as a person."

Be Aware of Mirroring

This is the unconscious replication of the other person's non-verbal signals. This non-verbal communication often goes unnoticed because we don't even realize we are doing it, and the other person doesn't realize it is happening. It is very subtle.

For example, if you are sitting across from someone and they cross their legs, you unconsciously may do the same a few minutes later. When someone mirrors you, they are probably trying to build a rapport, or they are unconsciously attracted to your body language. Your non-verbal cues make you interesting to the other person, so they want to act like you.

HOW TO READ AGGRESSION

Aggression is being forceful or attacking with or without provocation. The readiness to confront indicates that there may be more emotions than meets the eye. There are four types of aggression:

- Accidental aggression
- Instrumental aggression
- Expressive aggression
- Hostile aggression

Accidental aggression:

Accidental aggression is when you hurt another person without meaning to. For example, you may accidentally step on another person's foot or hit another person in the face when putting on your coat sleeve. You did not mean to be aggressive, but you accidentally hurt someone else.

Instrumental aggression:

This is where you and the other person fight over territory, objects, or rights, and in trying to get to these items first, the other person gets hurt. It is about control, and most outbursts between people are typically over material things. This type of aggression usually indicates a lack of maturity and poor development of cognitive skills.

Hostile aggression:

Hostile aggression is done on purpose to hurt the other person psychologically or physically. People who engage in this type of aggression derive satisfaction from seeing other people suffer because they feel more powerful. Unprovoked hostile aggression is also known as bullying.

But there is another side to hostile aggression, known as reactive aggression. This is whereby after provocation, you react aggressively to defend yourself and/or others.

Expressive aggression:

People engage in expressive aggression because it makes them feel good, but they do not intend their actions to hurt other people. Contact sports are a typical example of expressive aggression. For example, you may love to box because hitting something helps you de-stress. This is expressive aggression.

Signs of aggression:

- Bullying
- Physical acts of confrontation against others
- Gossiping and exclusion of others (psychological aggression)
- Ignoring others on purpose (Psychological aggression)
- Verbal abuse

HOW TO READ DEFENSIVENESS

Defensiveness is a natural response to the feeling of someone being critical of you. As a result of this feeling, we behave in a harsh, aggressive manner to protect ourselves from the intrusion. The defensive behavior distracts us from feeling criticized, so we shift attention to the other person to feel less vulnerable.

Usually, defensiveness is caused by existing insecurities, trauma, abuse, anxiety, shame, guilt, a health disorder, learned behavior, or helplessness.

Signs of defensiveness:

- Sarcasm
- Silent treatment
- Being critical in return
- Stop listening to the other person
- Justification and righteous indignation
- Bringing up the past
- Avoid talking about the current problem
- Belittling the feelings of the other person
- Gaslighting

Unfortunately, defensive behaviors don't work because as we attack and criticize the other person, we end up making them feel defensive as well, leaving us all stuck in a cycle of defensiveness.

HOW TO READ NERVOUSNESS

Nervousness in communication occurs when one party is worried, fearful, or anxious about communicating with the other party. It is usually a normal reaction, but it can become excessive and hamper the flow of communication.

Signs of nervousness:

- Rapid breathing
- Profuse sweating
- Pacing up and down
- Fidgeting with any item close to you
- Biting or picking at your nails
- Continuous and rapid rubbing of the upper arms like you are feeling cold
- Rocking or swaying
- Cracking the knuckles
- Tapping with your fingertips
- Avoiding eye contact
- Darting eyes
- Blinking continuously
- Trembling voice and hands

- Skin looking flushed

HOW TO READ BOREDOM

Boredom during communication occurs when the conversation does not offer us satisfaction. That means it is not stimulating enough, and we are not intrigued by what we are hearing or learning. Boredom indicates that the bored party is not fully engaged or present or that the conversation is not meaningful enough.

Boredom in communication occurs when we are forced to do something we do not want to be involved in, like attending a seminar. If we do not attach meaning to the communication process, we do not value it. Typically boredom manifests as irritation or lethargy.

There are five types of boredom:

Calibrating boredom: This is where you do not know what to do with yourself. You do not have the motivation to find something better to do, so you are stuck communicating with someone, but if something better comes up, you have the energy to get involved and pursue it. You will probably leave the date to go and hang out with friends. This type of boredom is common with first dates and blind dates.

Indifferent boredom: This is relaxing boredom that doesn't make you restless. Your mind is partially on the conversation, and you even get involved once in a while when you hear something that interests you. This type of boredom is prevalent in classroom settings or company presentations. Once in a while, the teacher will ask you a question, and you will participate and answer it.

Reactant boredom: Reactant boredom is characterized by tension, fidgetiness, and a desperate need to escape the boring environment. You can easily become angry with the person you are communicating with and blame them for putting you in that position of boredom. This boredom is common in babysitting experiences or when adults are paired with children for a task, like at a children's party.

Searching boredom: Searching boredom is the most proactive of all types of boredom. You feel bored, but instead of getting frustrated by the feeling, you search for something to do that you enjoy. However, the trick lies in finding something constructive to do and not indulging in destructive behaviors.

Apathetic boredom: This is depressive boredom that is associated with depression. It makes you feel extremely unhappy, but you do not have the energy to pull yourself out of that sunken place.

Depending on your conversation with the other party, you can tell what kind of boredom they are experiencing.

Signs of Boredom:

- Nodding off
- Unexcited responses
- Yawning
- Inability to remain interested in the communication process for longer than brief periods
- Inability to relax or rest
- No enthusiasm for life
- Difficulty in staying motivated

HOW TO READ ENGAGEMENT

Engagement is active with the participation of both the listener and speaker. It connects and requires good faith to work. Engagement is actually more than communication. It is listening to understand the content, reflect on it and make relevant changes as a result.

For example, most people associate the word engagement with a man going on one knee, proposing, and producing a ring. The recipient of the ring says yes, and voila! They are engaged.

But engagement has a deeper meaning. It is a time to show commitment to each other and deepen your communication for further understanding to create a strong foundation for your marriage. This is what engagement should be across the board.

Signs of engagement:

- Nodding
- Eye contact
- Smile
- Going the extra mile
- Being collaborative
- Being responsible and reliable

TIPS ON USING BODY LANGUAGE EFFECTIVELY

- Smile when talking to other people, where appropriate, of course, as it helps make you approachable and relatable.

- Make eye contact because it shows you have nothing to hide and you are connecting with the other person's message. Steady eye contact shows confidence.

- Watch your posture to ensure you are not slouching, which makes it look like you are bored. Depending on the person you are talking to, you should either sit up straight, lean forward a little, or get down on your haunches for kids so your eyes are at the same level.

- Keep your hands in front of you and on the table with interlaced fingers

- If you are standing, keep your hands on your sides and stand upright

- Try to take up as much space as possible to keep an open stance. Cramming yourself into small spaces means you have to fold yourself, which makes you seem like you are trying to be small.

- Do not fidget or tap your fingers when talking to family and friends. That is because when you need to turn these gestures off during an important meeting, you will not be able to, which will communicate nervousness to the other party you are communicating with.

- Always walk calmly and slowly to show confidence. Hurried, breathless walking makes you look nervous or agitated, which is not good if you are meeting someone for a conversation. Think of it this way; "How many times have you seen a CEO or President running to catch the door before it closes?" They let it close and then open it again when they reach it. In fact, they move deliberately with poise and confidence, which is reassuring for anyone watching them. Avoid panicky movements.

- Wear a welcoming facial expression that is calm and at ease. Avoid clenching your jaw, speaking through your teeth, looking tense, or wrinkling your face. Have you ever looked at the expressions of Dwayne "The Rock" Johnson, the famous wrestler? When he wants to be intimidating, he draws his brows together while raising one of them, lets his nostrils flare, and tightens his mouth. On the other hand, during interviews, he has a welcoming face with relaxed facial muscles, a wide bright-eyed smile, and great eye contact.

- Dress appropriately according to the setting. Do not go to a wedding in office attire, and do not go to the office in an evening gown or tuxedo. Also, being over-dressed for an interview is always better than being underdressed. Shorts and a t-shirt for a managerial interview will cost you the job. For ladies, avoid loud, colorful clothes that take the attention away from the communication process and onto you for all the wrong reasons.

- Speak gently and with consideration for others around you. Do not be too loud, and practice discretion even when you are surprised or caught off guard in a moment. For example, do not curse or hoot with laughter. Your actions during the conversation reflect not only on you but on the other person as well, and you do not want to make them stand out in a public place for all the wrong reasons.

- Have a firm handshake that is not too hard and not limp either. Some people believe a firm handshake squeezes the life out of the other person's hand, but that is not the case. It should be a medium grip with a gentle up and down motion. If you do this right, the other person will not think twice about your handshake. But when you don't get it right, the handshake will be the focal point of the other party's engagement with you. Practice with your parents and siblings to ensure you get it right.

Remember, we can see body language right from the moment you walk into a room. And our communication feeds off each other's body language and energy.

6

THE MIRACLE OF EMPATHY

E mpathy is the capacity to understand what another person is going through and sense their emotions.

"Learning to stand in somebody else's shoes, to see through their eyes, that's how peace begins. And it's up to you to make that happen. Empathy is a quality of character that can change the world."

— BARACK OBAMA

It definitely changes the communication process.

TYPES OF EMPATHY

There are three types of empathy. We will explore each and the skills you need to practice them:

Cognitive Empathy

This is also known as perspective-taking empathy. It is where you are listening to the other person to take in their perspective so that you can understand their point of view better. It allows you to put yourself in another person's shoes but not necessarily feel their emotions.

Example of cognitive empathy:

Interrogators who torture others exhibit cognitive empathy, where they can put themselves in their victims' shoes to know where it hurts the most but without exhibiting sympathetic emotions toward them.

Emotional Empathy

This is considered an intense type of empathy because you feel the other person's pain and can relate to their distress. It is as if you are the one experiencing the emotions. Whereas cognitive empathy is empathy by thought, emotional empathy is empathy by feeling. It is also known as emotional contagion because the other person's feelings of distress are contagious.

The good side of emotional empathy is that it allows us to readily understand and accept the feelings of others. This quality is incredibly important in caring professions, like in the healthcare industry. The flip side is that this type of empathy can introduce you to feelings that overwhelm you. If you are prone to this type of empathy, it is critical to learn self-control so that these emotions do not overwhelm you.

Example of emotional empathy:

When a mother smiles at her baby and the baby feels the mother's warmth and love and smiles back.

When the grief of a bereaved person touches you so deeply that you find yourself crying along with them.

Compassionate Empathy

This is considered the best type of empathy because it causes you to feel the other person's pain and find ways to resolve it for them. The additional move to take action regarding the other party's situation brings the compassion full circle. In most cases, people need compassionate empathy more than emotional or cognitive empathy.

People may not want your overwhelming emotional reaction to their pain or your disconnected reaction to their pain. They want your understanding and a possible way forward to find the best way out of the situation. Cognitive empathy is considered under-emotional, emotional empathy is overly emotional, but compassionate empathy is a balance between logic and emotion.

Examples of compassionate empathy:

When you see a young mother overwhelmed by caring for their child, and you offer to babysit so they can get some rest.

When you see someone injured and you take action, bringing them to a hospital or calling for an ambulance.

Two other types of empathy exist. One is spiritual empathy, which allows us to connect with a higher being and consciousness. It also allows us to do the right thing and act with kindness and consideration toward others. The other empathy is somatic empathy which allows us to feel other people's pain. Twins have been known to feel somatic empathy. When one of them gets hurt, the other one feels their pain.

HOW TO EMPATHIZE

Learn to get other people's perspectives:

To feel for the other person, you need to learn to use your imagination and put yourself in their shoes. But don't only use your imagination but also draw from your real-world experience in another similar experience.

It is very important to realize that the other person has a unique perspective and respect it even if it is far removed from yours. Even among family and friends, perspectives will change depending on the life experiences each of you goes through. Be open to hearing all perspectives because that increases understanding.

Remember that the same message can be interpreted very differently by two people in the same space. How you interpret a message is dependent on your mindset. For example, the message can come across as hostile if you are upset and teasing when you are happy.

Actually, misunderstanding other people's perspectives comes from the assumption that we all see things the same way. For example, we may assume that we all like music, but some people love sports over music.

Understanding each other's perspectives opens the mind to adopting helpful mindsets.

Avoid being Judgmental

Being Judgmental means you are quick to form opinions about other people and situations without considering all the information. And because of this, you become critical of others without the full picture. When we are judgmental, we do not show respect for the other person and quickly justify our perspective because we believe we are right and they are wrong.

Judgmental people have three predominant traits: Criticalness, pride, and closed-mindedness.

Critical people like to criticize everything about others. Nothing is good enough for them as long as it doesn't meet their usually unrealistic standards. And as long as we feel we are right, we become prideful and close our minds to other perspectives.

When we are judgmental, it becomes impossible to communicate with others because we tend to feel that they are beneath us and our righteous stands. Also, it becomes difficult to empathize because the other person's pain must be because of what they did or did not do. So they do not deserve your empathy.

Recognize Other People's Pain

Many people are walking around masking their pain. We wear masks daily, so the world thinks we are okay, but we are hurting inside. So when you communicate with others and notice signs of pain, do not ignore them. Allow yourself to recognize other people's pain and gently coax them to open up if you can. If not, talk to someone they trust and love to follow up with the signs.

We live in a world that tells us to mind our own business and so often forget to be each other's keepers. Statistics show that younger age groups have lower suicide rates compared to middle-aged adults and the elderly. Interestingly, the most vulnerable age group is the one that should have the most experience with communication because they have had more life experience.

How to Recognize Pain in Others

- Listen when people say they are unhappy
- Notice listlessness and lethargy
- Address your concerns about the concerned person's mental state and take action
- Find out what is happening in the background

THE ROLE OF EMPATHY IN COMMUNICATION

Empathic communication accepts and allows different perspectives enabling people to feel free to show their real emotions around you. This is a key component of emotional intelligence, but it doesn't come automatically to everyone. However, developing empathic communication is key to becoming a formidable leader, wherever you are. The best part is that you can use empathic listening in all spheres of your life, not just in crises.

Empathic communication allows you to:

- **Give your full attention to others**

This entails actively listening, using your eyes, and following your gut. That is how you recognize other people's pain and telltale signs of underlying emotions. It enables you to fully understand the entire message the sender is giving you.

To give full attention, begin by listening to keywords and phrases that they use which appear in the conversation repeatedly. Also, what is the tone of voice, gestures, posture, facial expressions, and eyes? Sometimes listening and communicating empathically means you hold your questions, arguments, or disputing facts at this stage so you can hear more than what is being said verbally.

- **Explore other people's perspectives**

You cannot grow by just looking at your own perspective. Empathic communication means that you are open to hearing the other side of the argument and are okay with agreeing to disagree. Allowing other people's perspectives to exist doesn't diminish you. Conversely, if you never allow others to have a different perspective from you, you become closed-minded and a bully.

- **Take Action**

When you engage in empathic communication, you are compelled to do something to alleviate the other person's pain, even if it is just offering a shoulder to cry on. Sometimes the action is just listening and understanding, depending on their dominant emotion at the time. After all, empathy is not about you but the other party and what they need from you. If you cannot offer it, then be straightforward and let them know.

Empathy in Action During Communication

- Smiling at someone who is feeling bashful and is looking for a lifeline so they do not feel alone in the crowd

- Being genuinely curious about people and their lives in a positive way

- Offering constructive criticism when asked for it

- Being fully present during meetings and giving the speaker your full attention

- Being interested in other people's cultures and hobbies

- Visiting with friends who are bereaved or have family in the hospital

7

STORM OF EMOTIONS

Negative emotions are part of life, and they profoundly affect our communication style, from verbal to body language. Below are some of the stormy emotions we experience daily, how they affect our communication and how to deal with them.

ANGER

Anger is an antagonistic emotion toward someone else or a situation, and it is typically associated with negative feelings that affect communication by creating a hostile environment. There are three types of anger which are:

Passive anger: This is when we are angry but don't like to admit or act on it in confrontation. That type of anger is called passive aggression, which is present and even tangible, but we do not act on it. Instead, we show anger through everyday actions like sarcastic speech, how we handle objects, and our attitude. Passive anger involves pretending to be okay, but we have anger simmering in everything we do.

Open anger: This is when we openly show our anger and lash out at people and situations. It results in becoming verbally or physically aggressive. Open anger manifests as physical fights, blackmail, shouting, yelling, throwing things, bullying, bickering, and criticism. People who manifest open anger tend to need to control their environment and feel vulnerable when they don't, so they become angry.

Assertive anger: Assertive anger is a mixture of controlled and confident anger. It allows us to listen more and talk less, even when angry. As a result, we think more about what we are about to say so we do not worsen the situation by saying something that adds fuel to the fire. Assertive anger:

- Is patient
- Keeps emotions in check
- Doesn't raise the voice
- Articulates the issues
- Looks for a solution

Dealing with Anger:

- All the above tips listed in assertive anger help to deal with anger.

FEAR

Fear is being afraid, and it is an emotion triggered by the perception of a threat or danger. This emotion makes it harder to regulate our emotions because it interrupts brain signals that regulate some of our actions, like thinking before acting and being ethical despite fear.

The fear associated with anticipated or real conversations with other people results in communication apprehension. While communication apprehension is psychological, it manifests in physical symptoms like sweating profusely, trembling, nausea, and poor concentration, among other things.

Dealing with Fear:

Unfortunately, we receive terrible advice about how to deal with communication apprehension. But to deal with fear, do not buy into the following misconceptions:

- Do not feel like you are neurotic or abnormal for experiencing communication apprehension. It is more common than you think.

- Do not imagine the crowd naked (It doesn't work). Plus, there are some people you respect too much to want to see naked.

- Do not try to memorize your conversation or speech. The pressure of trying to recollect everything word for word increases communication apprehension.

- Accept mistakes because no communication is perfect. For example, if you use "he" instead of "she" when referring to a female, it is not the end of the world. Bounce back by correcting yourself and moving on.

- It is better to get straight to the point and avoid making jokes at the beginning of the conversation. Jokes can be well received or not, and if yours is poorly received, then your apprehension is amplified.

- Do not imagine the audience can see your nervousness. Typically, the audience cannot see much of our nervousness unless we begin to act out nervous behavior.

- Embrace nervousness because it may help you give an even better speech. If you ask most expert public speakers and communicators, they prefer to have some nervousness because when they stop feeling it, they lose their edge.

SADNESS

Sadness is the feeling of emotional pain or being upset. Fortunately, sadness is temporary and fades with time unless it is an indicator of an underlying condition that causes the feeling to become overwhelming and all-consuming, interfering with daily life. Sadness increases pessimism, lethargy, and depression, making it hard for people to communicate and connect with others when in this state. We cannot be bothered to maintain friendships when consumed by such a negative, all-consuming emotion.

Dealing with Sadness:

Whether it is you or someone else feeling sad, here are a few tips on how to deal with this emotion:

- Be patient and understanding with others and yourself

- Acknowledge gains made to move away from sadness, no matter how small

- If there is a mental health condition, acknowledge it but realize that it is not your fault or the other person's fault

- Focus on what you can do today to feel better or what you can do for the other person to make them feel better.

LONELINESS

Loneliness is a feeling of isolation despite wanting to have social interactions. Sometimes the feeling of isolation is in our minds and not physical. And sometimes, it can mean being alone physically. When we feel lonely, we are less open to communication, so we hide personal information because we are afraid of judgement for being a loner. Unfortunately, lonely people fare worse in social interactions.

Dealing with Loneliness:

- Step out of your comfort zone, so do not stay at home. Instead, go and shoot hoops at the community center.

- Step out of your routine. Instead of leaving work or school and going straight home, invite a friend for coffee or go to the gym.

- Volunteer at the local shelter or do something great for your community but make sure it is not a solitary action. For example, you can volunteer to farm at the local agricultural plot together with other volunteers.

- Join a class to learn something you are interested in, like baking, origami, or repairing classic vehicles.

- Find support online. Online connections were really helpful for mental health and for keeping communication going during the COVID pandemic. So many groups have opened up exceptional communication avenues, such as Facebook groups, fitness groups, and other meet-up groups.

ANNOYANCE

Annoyance is the same as irritation. When irritated, it becomes difficult to communicate with others because their response could be triggering. Vexation can be a result of the actions of others or recurring situations.

Dealing with Annoyance:

- Avoid the trigger

- Think positively to dissipate the negative feelings

- Be self-aware and self-reflect.

REJECTION/CRITICISM/ DISAPPROVAL

Criticism is an expression of disapproval that results in rejection. It is difficult to want to communicate with others when you feel like you are not wanted based on perceived mistakes or faults. All the above feelings make it hard to want to be vulnerable to others in a conversation.

Dealing with rejection/criticism/ disapproval:

- Remain calm even when facing criticism

- Avoid being critical of the person

- Pay attention to signs of all the above, and if you can, remove yourself from the situation to do some self-reflection

- As hard as it is, listen to what the other person is saying to see if there is any truth

- Do not take being rejected, excluded, or ignored personally

HELPLESSNESS

Helplessness is a feeling of being unable to protect yourself. Unfortunately, we learn this behavior and become conditioned to believe that the bad situation is unchangeable. When we feel this vulnerable, we cannot communicate effectively because we fall into the zone of "I'm not okay – You are okay." We are caught up in a victim mentality.

The good news is that we can learn optimism.

Dealing with Helplessness:

- Explore the origins of this learned helplessness

- Identify the negative triggers that cause the helplessness

- Go for therapy where necessary because unlearning some behaviors may be very challenging on your own.

- Learn to communicate positively with others to improve optimism and positivity

8

FEEDBACK IN COMMUNICATION

As mentioned earlier, the communication process includes three important components:

- The sender
- The message
- The receiver

Receivers don't receive messages passively; they respond to the messages received. The act of a receiver responding to a sender's message is called feedback. We may offer feedback in written form, like replying to an email, text, writing a letter, etc. It can also be non-verbal with smiles and sighs, facial expressions, gestures, or verbal, as in reacting to someone's ideas with comments or questions.

Your audience responds through feedback which allows you to gauge the effectiveness of your message. If your message doesn't get through to your audience, you can tell from their response and clarify the message accordingly. To create a climate of open communication, it is crucial to provide a conducive environment for your audience to give feedback. For example, a manager must create an atmosphere that encourages feedback in the work environment. After issuing instructions to a team member, the manager must confirm if they have been understood or not and if there are any doubts. Team members must also be free to express their views. Communication is perceived to be successful if the messages sent by the sender are interpreted with the same meaning by the receiver.

Feedback is crucial in communication to determine whether the recipient has understood the message as purposed by the sender, and whether they agree with the message.

One vital component of the personal growth of an individual is feedback. Humans require feedback to continue improving their lives and that of those around them. In an environment void of feedback, people fail to reach their full potential. Feedback helps us develop our mental fitness, learn, grow and try new ideas.

In a working environment, employees require feedback that supports skill building. A survey carried out by Deloitte Global Millennial shows that one of the top considerations for leaving employment among employees is failure to offer leadership and skills development.

Most people are uncomfortable giving feedback, especially if it is negative, because they don't want to come across as being judgmental of others. Although feedback might, in most cases, appear critical, that should not be the case when done correctly. There are different types of feedback that serve different purposes. Ultimately when expressed correctly, feedback is highly valuable.

Feedback equips you with the information you didn't have and allows you to see things outside the box. In fact, feedback that builds your effectiveness is a precious gift.

In this book, we shall delve into different types of feedback, how they can be applied in an organization and why feedback is beneficial. In the workplace, feedback naturally shows up in more ways than you can imagine. Here are three scenarios where the common flow of feedback at the workplace is at work:

- A team member might develop a new, faster, and more efficient process

- The team leadership could reward a member for their hard work

- The leadership could have a discussion with an employee to help rein them in for not adhering to their roles and responsibilities.

All of the above three scenarios are a reflection of some type of feedback. A common misconception that needs to be rebutted is that feedback is always negative or bad. If anything, feedback should be viewed as a sign of concern and care and that someone has personally invested in the growth and development of an individual or a corporation.

When support systems such as coaching and mentorship are applied, feedback is key in unlocking human potential. There are various types of feedback that anyone can deliver. Let's now look at who can provide feedback.

WHO CAN PROVIDE FEEDBACK?

The word feedback provokes memories of someone in our personal or professional journeys. Feedback can come from a wide range of people we interact with, including a friend, family members, partners, colleagues, bosses, teachers, and so on. We are continually receiving feedback from the people around us all the time, and we should be alert so that we do not let it slip away unnoticed.

However, feedback is most useful when it is structured. Structured feedback means it is normalized, high quality, well-intentioned, and occurs close to the moment of the communication or event.

In the workplace, feedback tends to be driven by the following:

Team Members: Peers can provide regular feedback in the workplace. They can review your work and provide advice, recommendations, and new ideas on areas of improvement. Peer-to-peer feedback is critical communication for any working relationship. When properly harnessed, it can build trust and expand innovation, collaboration, and creativity.

Managers: The words "manager" and "feedback" tend to go hand in hand, making them synonymous. Feedback is a key tool in any managerial or supervisory work. Managers are expected to deliver both positive and negative feedback to their team members, but they are expected to apply their managerial skills when doing it. They should be careful so that the feedback can be received positively to improve the team members and the organization at large.

Customers: Customer feedback is key for any organization's growth. According to a survey done by Forbes, 77% of consumers are attracted to brands that seek out and respond to customer feedback. Without customer feedback, services and products are likely to be rendered irrelevant. You can only be sure a business is enjoying some market share by meeting your customers' needs and getting feedback on how satisfied they are and the available opportunities to expand your business.

Leadership Team: The leadership team is critical in the feedback process. In most cases, their feedback is more valuable. Considering where they are positioned between the stakeholders or top management and the employees or junior staff, the leadership team can gather a lot of valuable feedback.

Coach/Mentor: Your coach is your direction pointer and cheerleader. A coach can't succeed in molding a person in an environment devoid of feedback. Coaches guide you based on the feedback reflected by your words and behavior. They provide feedback that supports reflection in ways that bring out your inconsistencies and ineffectiveness. Through feedback, a coach can push you out of your comfort zone and help you navigate different situations.

THE IMPORTANCE OF FEEDBACK IN COMMUNICATION

Feedback is critical to the communication process. It illustrates the missing link in the sender-receiver loop. A two-way communication process is summed up by feedback. Here are the reasons why we should value feedback:

- The only way you can confirm a message has been received by the recipient and understood in the terms intended by the sender is through feedback.

- Continuous learning thrives on feedback.

- Constructive feedback is a motivation to the sender.

- Communication barriers between the sender and receiver are eliminated through feedback.

- Feedback greatly improves human relations, which is considered a vital communication skill.

- The level of effective communication between two parties is reflected through feedback.

Feedback in the workplace

In the workplace, feedback provides vital information or constructive criticism about the company or its staff. Effective feedback is a priceless asset for any business.

The feedback received by companies from their clients, stakeholders, suppliers, and employees can determine the action to be taken by the company to improve its performance. Regardless of whether it is positive or negative feedback, a brand can leverage the feedback it receives to its advantage.

Clients' needs are well captured through customer feedback creating new growth opportunities for the company and offering a competitive edge in the respective market. Customer feedback also creates a sense of clients being valued while maintaining healthy communication levels.

Employee Feedback

Eliminates confusion and ambiguity and gives the management more insight into the company's inner workings than the analytics will show. Employee feedback brings out the sense of being valued and brings to the fore the business's good and bad elements.

Regular feedback on employee performance

This can greatly increase employee motivation. We can attain high efficiency and work-related accomplishments through constructive evaluation and frequent feedback. Feedback helps coordinate different departments so that the top-tier management is kept abreast of what is happening in the organization.

The company's overall performance can be greatly boosted by understanding the stakeholder's feedback. Feedback improves the in-house relationship between the CEO, managers, and employees. Constant exchange of feedback has been used as a tool world over by companies to solve problems. Feedback is vital for the proper functioning of any business.

WHY IS FEEDBACK CRUCIAL?

Feedback is required because:

- It completes a two-way communication loop between the sender and receiver.

- It can gauge the effectiveness of communication. From the feedback, the sender can be sure the receiver properly understood the message.

- The success or failure of communication can be determined by the feedback.

- Efficient feedback enables the sender to decide on the next course of action.

- By communicating the receiver's thoughts to the sender, the feedback aids the sender in taking the next best decision.

We can now summarize the importance of feedback in communication by saying the importance of feedback in communication cannot be disapproved. Irrespective of the message being communicated, feedback will elevate the discussion to the next level.

Feedback avails an opportunity for the parties involved in communicating to understand more about their level of communication needs and desires.

Feedback is the focal point in the communication process. Collecting feedback is only part of the journey because what matters most is how the collected information is integrated and returned to the sender.

TYPES OF FEEDBACK

Different types of feedback serve distinctive purposes. Let's review the types of feedback applied in an organization. There are 5 types of feedback, namely:

- Constructive feedback
- Upward feedback
- Appreciation and recognition
- Coaching feedback
- Real-time feedback

Constructive Feedback

Studies indicate that most people perceive constructive feedback as negative, even though they believe this feedback improves performance. For example, an employee might miss a few details on a current project. Due to the workload involving other projects that the employee is currently involved in, the manager may ignore the mistakes. As the projects that the employee handles reduce, the manager may still notice the recurrence of the same mistakes. In the next one-on-one meeting with the employee, the manager should raise the issues of concern. The manager can start by addressing what the employee is doing well, followed by areas in which the employee needs to improve. This is where the manager offers some constructive feedback about the trend of mistakes. Finally, the manager should conclude with positive feedback. This method of constructive feedback is known as a feedback sandwich. The manager should then find out how the employee wants to be assisted in overcoming their weaknesses. The employee is likely to express gratitude and request further professional development.

A request from an employee for feedback is usually for constructive feedback. Listen carefully and zero in on the exact area the employee requires feedback on and to what level.

Upward Feedback

Upward feedback is when a manager requests feedback from their direct reports. It is a key aspect of feedback that is shunned in some organizations. If an organization values employee experience and believes that staff voices need to be heard, then managers requesting feedback from their employees are promoting a culture of feedback. Feedback culture promotes psychological safety and real change, and it gives staff some impetus and improves the work environment and relationships among staff.

Upward feedback helps a manager meet employees' needs because it allows a manager to understand each of the employee's challenges and how to overcome them.

Appreciation and Recognition

Feedback is not always negative. Appreciation and employee recognition are critical in getting your employee involved. Organizations that frequently appreciate and recognize their employees are better in terms of performance, internal relationships, and higher job satisfaction.

Coaching Feedback

Pairing up with a coach is a way of unlocking potential through feedback. Coaching feedback creates an atmosphere where the coach serves as a guide for the employee and does not pose any threats. In coaching feedback, we have a unique and collaborative environment. Individuals can feel intimidated when they receive feedback, leading to imposter syndrome and insecurities. Negative thoughts like loss of job and lack of promotion can creep in. With a coach, employees feel safe asking for help and requesting feedback. The coach is immediately perceived as a teammate. Studies show that coaching results in a reduction in stress levels, an increase in resilience and job performance, and improved focus in staff.

Real-time Feedback

The new performance management tools have made it easier to provide both negative and positive feedback in real time. This kind of feedback can be used to address challenges arising out of day-to-day tasks.

5 TIPS FOR PROVIDING FEEDBACK

Think about what your feedback will achieve.

What do you want to achieve? Is it changing a behavior, improving a relationship, or fixing something urgently? These questions can lead you to a suitable type of feedback you would like to provide.

Empathy and kindness: No matter the type of feedback you provide, you need to demonstrate empathy and kindness. Feedback is a demonstration of care and compassion. The success and well-being of the person getting the feedback is paramount, and the aim is to ensure they realize their full potential.

Listen carefully: The recipient of the feedback might have issues they want to be clarified. Ensure you listen more than you talk to allow the recipient to ask questions. You might get an insight into the recipient's approach to issues. Failure to listen results in miscommunication and misunderstanding of expectations. Let your employees be alive to the fact that you care about their perspectives.

Offer support: Depending on the feedback provided, you will want to follow through by extending support. This support is in the form of professional development through, say, virtual coaching. It could also be a skill-sharpening and learning opportunity in the form of an online course or workshop. In other cases, a follow-up on the previous meeting can help clarify expectations and answer questions. Whatever the circumstances, provide your support and demonstrate your desire for the success of your employees or the recipient of the feedback. This creates an environment where employees feel cared for and valued.

Clear and concise: Avoid a situation whereby the recipient of the feedback is not sure what the feedback is about. Direct, concise, and clear communication is key, and it is essential to get to the core of the matter promptly and directly while ensuring there is time and space to allow feedback absorption.

Get into the culture of giving feedback: Feedback should not wait for performance review, and for it to be effective, it doesn't have to be negative. In an environment void of feedback, people tend to come up with haphazard solutions which might not eventually be helpful. Allow employees to be on the same page and know what you think. Avoid creating an environment for your employee's worst interpretations and anxieties. Feedback is of great significance in the workplace. There is a wide range of feedback types to choose from, each serving its own unique purpose – whether you are dealing with employee performance or conflict resolution.

Good feedback is achieved over time and is a learning process that takes practice. Providing feedback is a daunting task, but with proper support like coaching, an organization can develop a structured evaluative feedback model.

Remember, any kind of feedback can be used to spur growth in an organization, unlocking human potential and promoting passion, clarity, and purposeful life among employees.

HOW TO RECEIVE FEEDBACK

Giving and receiving feedback can be intimidating, and it is something people often try to run away from.

Feedback is important, and getting better at it will:

- Provide an opportunity to see the real-life strengths and weaknesses so that you can better harness the strengths and improve in areas that require development.

- Give the people you interact with an opportunity to develop in their areas of weakness and apply their strengths to their advantage.

- Build relationship quality and trust by avoiding miscommunication which in turn allows for more honest and forthright conversations.

- Polishing the art of giving and receiving feedback will hasten your development and that of those you interact with. It will help you build trust, a key component in relationships, making you more influential.

Feedback is far from a performance review. The feedback we are addressing here is the informal sharing that takes place daily, not the periodic organizational performance review. This daily informal feedback can never be replaced by an annual performance review. The two function differently: Daily feedback supports an individual's development which is a work in progress, while a performance review is put in place to meet the expectations of an organizational system. In informal daily feedback conversations, whatever is raised in an organizational performance review should have been discussed multiple times. Surprises should never spring up in a formal performance review.

Giving and Receiving Feedback

Giving and receiving feedback well are two key elements of an effective feedback process. It is critical to note that for your feedback to be more influential, you need to listen consistently to the feedback you receive. Proficiency in feedback begins with listening well.

Active listening

Active listening is the most refined and influential form of listening. When correctly done, active listening:

- Calls for maximum attention to focus on what is being said, preventing you from thinking about the response.

- Gets to confirm that whatever is being said is what is meant by providing a sense check for the speaker.

- Completes the process by making the speaker understand what you have grasped from the communication.

Active listening is a demonstration of your commitment to the existing relationship. By being attentive to what they are communicating, you clearly show the significance you attach to what they are saying.

Active listening demonstrates that you are not emotionally attached to what you hear, and it means you do not pass judgement on what you are hearing. How do you listen actively? You do so by summarizing the key messages communicated and reviewing them with the speaker briefly and comprehensively, without any emotions, even if they are present.

We can break it down into the following steps:

- **Identify the main concepts heard**: What was their most significant message?

- **Pick out any emotions present:** Are there any feelings relayed in this message? If so, what are they?

- **Summarise as concisely as possible**: What is the briefest message you can use to describe the most important message and the emotion therein?

- **Review with the speaker:** Share your brief content, including the emotional summary, with the speaker.

How to Receive Feedback

Active listening is the most important component of receiving feedback skillfully. Let's look at a five-step feedback receiving model:

1. Active listening (micro)

Once you realize you are about to receive feedback, it is imperative to commit to active listening to be effective in the interaction. This will benefit you in two ways.

Involving yourself in executing this vital skill engages your analytical brain to analyze the communication you are receiving, setting it apart from your emotional brain that may otherwise want to become defensive.

You will be too busy absorbing what you are hearing so that you can capture the message and any emotions therein, and wonder how to summarize it, and therefore you will have no time for an ill-judged response.

Micro-active listening involves summarizing each piece of what is said. After the first summary; additions, corrections, or clarifications to the communication can then take place. Then you summarize the next communication one after another until you are done.

2. Active listening (macro)

Once finished, in the second step you apply active listening again, but in this case, you summarize your entire interaction. Bring out your summary of the whole message and any emotions.

3. Thank and recognize the giver

It is of great significance that you should then thank the giver for the feedback shared. This should happen irrespective of whether the feedback is positive or negative or whether you agree with it or not. It's by establishing a reputation as someone sincerely interested in getting feedback that you set up a conducive environment where you continue receiving constructive feedback essential for your future growth. If you are thankless, the feedback provider is unlikely to try again, preventing you from accessing the priceless information.

For clear, specific, and understandable feedback, thanking them marks the conclusion of the process. If the feedback provider shared something you differed with, let it pass for now. Bring it up in a later interaction, or better still, let your subsequent actions speak for you.

4. Ask to probe

Sometimes the feedback received might not be clear or specific, and therefore you do not know what is expected of you to be more effective in the future. If this is the scenario, after honestly thanking the feedback provider, politely engage them by asking, "Is it okay with you if I ask you a question or two about your feedback"? If you get NO for an answer, perhaps steps 1-3 have not been handled effectively, in which case you need to revert to that step and start afresh.

5. Probe to understand

Once you get YES for an answer, you can then ask probing questions that will assist you to convert their lower-quality feedback into high-quality feedback. Possible questions include: "When you said I was not a team player, what specifically did I do that caused you to conclude that?" "When did that happen?" "What would you advise I should have done in that situation?"

Expanding a receiving feedback mindset

Understanding best practices when receiving feedback and getting the courage actually to practice this culture in real-life situations are two different ball games. This section is about enticing you to be courageous enough to reap the huge benefits of faster self-development and creating stronger relationships.

To effectively understand our true strengths and development areas in the world, we must be able to access a broad range of others' perspectives. This is an uncomfortable topic for most people, particularly supervisors.

Here are four real-life situations to encourage you to practice the culture of feedback from others.

- **All feedback is perception:**

Any single piece of feedback speaks more about the giver than the receiver. As human nature dictates, we are held captive by the filters and biases in our minds. In view of this, any feedback received is obscured more by the giver's filters than by your actual act. All feedback is nothing but perception. Feedback is an indication of the giver's filters rather than your actions or behavior; it is of great significance that you get feedback from multiple and various sources. With this approach, you can evaluate and come up with common themes from multiple sources that may warrant action.

- **People have already made up their minds:**

Most people have their impressions about something or someone already set in their minds. Avoiding feedback does not eradicate perceptions; it simply means you don't get to know people's perceptions of you. Everyone, including strangers, already has their opinions about you. Getting their feedback gives you an opportunity to hear what they think, and you can then decide to do something about it or not.

Your role in receiving feedback is to hear and acknowledge that the other party has a particular opinion. Accepting that they have an opinion does not mean you agree with it. Your role is to hear and acknowledge their opinion without being judgmental.

- **You don't always have to measure feedback:**

Another misunderstanding regarding feedback is that you need to act on it if you listen to it. This is a misconception, especially taking into consideration that any single piece of feedback says more about the giver's state of mind than the receiver. Most people value being heard, not what you subsequently choose to do with what they tell you. You build your relationship with someone when they feel you are willing to lend them your ear, which is attained by you listening without prejudice.

Whatever action you take as a result is upon you. We, however, recommend that you demonstrate the value you attach to their feedback by letting them know what you eventually did or did not do at a later date, giving reasons for taking or not taking action. The act of allowing them an audience is the most significant step you can take, even more important than your subsequent actions.

- **Asking for feedback:**

Some working environments do not encourage the culture of giving and receiving feedback. This is where the culture of sharing is shunned. Keep asking for feedback persistently and in a polite manner. Once you have created the habit and it is accepted, you can start asking for two, three, or four items of feedback.

How to Give Feedback

Feedback is two-way traffic. The same way that the feedback received needs to be heard to be effective, the feedback given also has to be heard. The difference is that when you are a recipient of feedback, you control the listening, and when you are giving feedback, you don't. In reality, your ability to make your feedback captivating essentially impacts whether your feedback is given an ear. This distinction is of great significance, because giving feedback as an act of influencing helps us achieve effectiveness, and so the feedback given needs to be heard in the simplest way possible.

10 best practice principles of giving feedback:

- **It is frequent, regular, and continuous:** It should happen all the time, with everybody, and about everything.

- **It should be genuine and truthful:** Your reputation hinges on being candid with people.

- **Offer an example:** Highlighting a specific example you noted enables the recipient to contextualize your feedback, making it easily understandable and more likely to respond to.

- **It should describe the good or bad impact of the behavior:** Hearing and getting to know the benefits or consequences of the behavior makes the recipient understand the importance of the feedback.

- **It should be timely:** Strive to share the feedback as close to the event as practically possible.

- **Own it:** Ensure there is clarity that the feedback emanated from you.

- **It should be concise**: Try to make feedback as brief as possible to achieve impact.

The above seven principles are applicable to all feedback, and the following three are applicable to developmental feedback only:

- **Focus on the future:** Express what you want to see going into the future rather than dwell on what you saw in the past.

- **Non-judgmental:** Focus on the behavior of the subject rather than the subject.

- **Shared privately:** Do not hurt the recipient's self-image or self-esteem and the existing relationship with them. Ensure that developmental conversations are carried out in private.

THE PERFORMANCE MANAGEMENT MODEL

Applying the Performance Management Model is the most beneficial way of identifying which feedback would be most helpful in a particular situation. In this model, feedback is segmented into three wide-ranging categories that correspond with the three levels of performance, namely excellent, acceptable and unacceptable.

Recognition Feedback

The most important motivational tool is recognition feedback. You give recognition feedback to motivate people to continue with excellent behavior. Honestly and authentically noticing people doing things right is your single most significant tool for:

- Promoting excellence for the recipient and the colleagues.

- Bettering their motivation and morale for both recipients and those who get to hear about it.

- Growing your relationships and gaining trust, which in turn strengthens your ability to influence. The best quality of a leader is noticing people who do things right and giving recognition for their excellent performance.

Improvement Feedback

The most important development tool is Improvement Feedback. You provide improvement feedback to a recipient whose behavior is acceptable for the purpose of improving their future performance. A matter of significance here is that improvement feedback improves acceptable behavior. Acceptable means the behavior comprises a mix of good and not-so-good things in their performance. To make the improvement feedback effective and as motivating as possible, share both the positive and negative aspects of the performance and ways of making improvements.

Confronting feedback

The confronting tool is the most important for setting expectations. You confront to put an end to the unacceptable or offending behavior and re-evaluate your expectations about future performance. Don't dwell on the past; instead, focus on the future. After all, the purpose of the confronting discussion is not to obtain an apology but to ensure all team players are reading from the same page regarding what your minimum acceptable standards are expected to look like heading forward. A major distinction about confronting is that the more you put it on the back burner, the more likely you will find yourself confronted by similar situations. Developing a reputation as one who engages respectfully in confrontational conversations will help you avoid a situation where things might spiral out of control.

The significance of agreed-upon expectations

Agreeing on expectations minimizes conflict through miscommunication and misunderstanding.

Expectation-eliciting questions at the beginning of every important interaction is a valuable investment. Every interaction should have a set of rules on how to agree to conduct selves while together. It is imperative to agree on the "dos and don'ts" and set rules of engagement in order to reduce the likelihood of conflict. Avoiding expectations in a relationship is a recipe for mismatched expectations and unstated assumptions. Both of which provide motivational challenges.

Feedback and relationship life stages

Reflecting on where you are in the life stage of a relationship can help you to prioritize what to focus on in terms of feedback. In the infancy of a relationship, bias toward honest recognition is beneficial as a means of hastening the fostering of the connection. Once the relationship is healthy with trust taking center stage, a leaning toward genuine improvement feedback will hasten development and foster the relationship because the recipient gains your commitment to their success.

9

WRITTEN COMMUNICATION

Written communication is an integral part of the communication landscape. Written communication is any written message exchanged between two or more people. This form of communication is more formal than verbal communication. There are several forms of written communication, including:

- Text messages
- Emails
- Business letters
- Blog posts
- Proposals
- Job descriptions
- Business letters
- Bulletins

- Employee manuals
- Reports
- Memos
- Postcards
- Advertisements
- Faxes
- Instant messages

You will notice that most of these are business-related forms of communication because most businesses rely on written communication to function.

QUALITIES OF EFFECTIVE WRITTEN COMMUNICATION

For written communication to be effective, it has to have the following qualities:

- **Be Comprehensible:**

That means that it should be easy to understand. Do not use complex language like jargon or complicated sentences: Keep it simple and understandable to get your message across.

- **Be Comprehensive:**

That means that the communication should include all the relevant information to the subject matter you are discussing. It is hard to make a decision or believe the communication if there are missing details.

- **Be Accurate:**

Whatever details, statistics, or facts you include in the communication should always be correct and accurate. Otherwise, your information will be unreliable, and no one will use your data in the future.

- **Be Grammatically Sound:**

When you write, you have to make sense to your reader, which is achieved by having grammatically sound sentences. A poorly written communication full of grammatical errors means you do not care to be careful and are not focused on your work. No one wants to read poorly written communication or to work hard to figure out what you are trying to say.

- **Have the Correct Tone:**

As mentioned earlier, written communication is more formal than verbal communication. So it is best to ensure that your communication has the correct levels of formality and the right. To achieve this, it is best to avoid using slang. Remember, you are not having a face-to-face conversation, so the other person cannot read your facial expressions and body language to decipher the communication better. In fact, they are wholly reliant on the exact words jumping off the page to them, so they may not get the "joke" or nuance that you are trying to communicate. Instead, it may read as a lack of seriousness.

- **Stay on Topic:**

Do not meander in your writing. For example, if you are writing a report addressing gender inequality at your workplace, do not veer off and begin to talk about the lack of standing desks and improvements needed in the cafeteria. Staying on the topic shows the reader that you are very singular in your purpose.

THE IMPORTANCE OF WRITTEN COMMUNICATION IN BUSINESS

- **It leaves a trail:**

Communication is about conveying messages and trusting another person's word when they tell it to you. Verbal communication can be denied because the words are not recorded automatically unless you record them on a device. However, written communication is a record of the exchange, and the trail can be used to ascertain facts about the communication when they are denied.

- **It is easier to distribute:**

Written communication can be easily distributed to more than one person, no matter where they are in the world. Verbal communication may need someone to be in the same vicinity as you. For example, a memo can be distributed widely in the company, while a meeting may require everyone's presence in the conference room, and everyone cannot make it for a physical meeting.

- **It represents you:**

Written communication helps you to stand out from the crowd. That is why making a good impression in all your written communications is important. If you are representing a company, you make your establishment look good. You will notice most companies require native English speakers to be the liaison with other companies, and poor grammar and sentence structure reflect the company.

With so many types of writing and editing software available, there is no excuse for having poor grammar or using words incorrectly in your written communication.

- **It establishes relationships:**

It is easier to remember people you have written communication with than those you have just spoken to. For example, if you have to talk to a fellow executive assistant, you must sign your name, title, telephone number, and other critical details. These details help humanize you and improve the chances of you being remembered.

There are four types of business written communication:

Informational communication

This is business-related communication that features informational materials, and it tends to provide a reference to a business-related record targeting specific aspects of the workplace.

Examples of informational communication:

- Employee handbooks
- Minutes from a meeting
- Financial reports
- Frequently asked questions on a website
- Departmental overviews

Transactional communication

This is communication involving a transaction between two or more parties, and it offers information pertinent to the transaction while also maintaining a business relationship. In this type of communication, it is not uncommon to come across negotiations and other transactional information.

Examples of transactional communication:

- Invoices
- Emails
- Memos
- Forms with personal information
- Letters, such as those between lawyers and their clients

Instructional communication

This communication gives instructions on how to carry out a task related to the business. It provides step-by-step details of the correct way to handle and complete a specific task. For instructional communication to be effective, the reader needs to understand the task well and what is expected of them. For example, you cannot send instructional communication to a layman to perform surgery.

That is communication that should take place between an attending doctor and an intern doctor.

Instructional communication features short, simple sentences which are in chronological order.

Examples of instructional communication:

- Manuals
- Instructional memos
- Technical specifications
- Descriptive handbooks

Persuasive Communication

This communication persuades others to complete a task or respond accordingly for the benefit of the business. Typically, sales material offers a proposition to the reader but can also be communicated to further a business relationship. This type of communication may not be too focused on the technicalities of the business, but instead, it focuses on the reader's pain points and how it can alleviate them. It offers solutions, and the writer tries to persuade the reader that they are the only ones who can offer this solution in the best way.

TIPS ON HOW TO MAINTAIN EFFECTIVE WRITTEN COMMUNICATION

- State your goal clearly from the initial sentences

- Maintain the right tone depending on whom you are writing to. For example, do not use slang in memorandums, but you can maintain a less formal tone when communicating with colleagues at the same level with emojis.

- Avoid jargon and unnecessarily complicated language. Simplicity is best in written communication. Even people with industry knowledge and experience do not understand all the jargon so keep it simple even when communicating with them. The last thing you want is to sound like a textbook and lose the human connection with your reader.

- Also, avoid unnecessary information by focusing on the topic of the communication. For example, do not start the communication with the company's long history when trying to make a sales pitch. The communication is to sell a product or service to the reader, not to tell them about every move your company has made over the last 50 years. The background is important sometimes, but if you have to give it, keep it brief and concise and ensure it works to your sales pitch's advantage.

- Use active voice instead of passive voice. Passive voice makes sentences harder to understand and awkward. It also tends to make the message's meaning vague, while the active voice makes the intention of the statements direct. Also, passive voice sentences are wordier than active voice sentences. Remember, you want your communication to feature short, simple sentences, not long, winding, convoluted sentences.

- Use short paragraphs, bullet points, and other writing elements that can make it easier for the reader to read. Large blocks of texts can be daunting to read and off-putting to your intended target, while paragraphs break down the content into manageable sections for reading.

- Proofread your own work, and then have someone else proofread it for you. A fresh set of eyes will always catch something that you didn't. And of course, there are many types of editing software on the market, so invest in one to ensure that your written work reads well.

- The trick to writing well is to practice. Practice your written communication over and over, at every opportunity. Over time your flow will get better, and communicating in written form will come more naturally to you.

EXAMPLES OF EFFECTIVE WRITTEN COMMUNICATION

Religious books: Whether you agree with their content or not, religious books have been passed down from generation to generation over centuries, and due to their simple message and clear wording, they have managed to impact people in the same way. Except for religious fanatics, religious texts call their followers to love each other and do good, which is why most people believe them. They also convey a message of hope and a better future.

Biographies and autobiographies: These are real accounts of people's lives based on facts, and they have continued to capture audiences' attention, making them some of the most popular books on the market. They are so compelling in written form that movie companies turn them into films to capture the visual aspects of these stories. Nelson Mandela's autobiography is an example of a written form of communication that communicated the struggle against apartheid and the strength of character of one man. Mandela captured his reader's attention by using simple language that they could understand and compelling words to communicate his experiences.

Here is an excerpt of communication that adhered to the rules of exceptional communication.

It is a speech by Mahatma Gandhi that was not only clear and concise, but also left those who were present with an understanding of the task at hand. It was the speech given on the eve of the Dandi March, also known as the Salt March. It had the following important communication elements:

- It stayed on topic from the beginning

- It was oratory and formal, which was important for the group he was addressing

- He used simple language that his audience could understand

- His tone was appropriate for the type of communication process

- He watched his language not only to allay fears, but also to avoid inciting violence in his supporters, considering the crowd at this gathering was over 10,000 people

- He offered a way forward for what he expected to happen in his absence

- He kept his body language neutral and his voice even

There were some grammatical errors, but the power of the speech and its communicator far surpassed these issues.

The Speech on the Eve of the Historic Dandi March

"In all probability, this will be my last speech to you. Even if the government allow me to march tomorrow morning, this will be my last speech on the sacred banks of the Sabarmati. Possibly these may be the last

words of my life here.

*I have already told you yesterday what I had to say.
Today I shall confine myself to what you should do
after my companions and I are arrested. The program
of the march to Jalapur must be fulfilled as originally
settled. The enlistment of the volunteers for this
purpose should be confined to Gujarat only. From
what I have been and heard during the last fortnight,
I am inclined to believe that the stream of civil
resisters will flow unbroken.*

*But let there be not a semblance of breach of peace
even after all of us have been arrested. We have
resolved to utilize all our resources in the pursuit of
an exclusively nonviolent struggle. Let no one commit
a wrong in anger. This is my hope and prayer. I wish
these words of mine reached every nook and corner of
the land. My task shall be done if I perish, and so do
my comrades. It will then be for the Working
Committee of the congress to show you the way, and it
will be up to you to follow its lead. So long as I have
reached Jalapur, let nothing be done in contravention
to the authority vested in me by congress. But once I
am arrested, the whole responsibility shifts to the
Congress. No one who believes in non-violence as a
creed, need therefore sit still. My compact with
congress ends as soon as I am arrested. In that case
volunteers. Wherever possible, civil disobedience of*

salt should be started. These laws can be violated in three ways. It is an offence to manufacture salt wherever there are facilities for doing so. The possession and sale of contraband salt, which includes natural salt or salt earth is also an offence. The purchasers of the salt are will be equally guilty. To carry away the natural salt deposits on the seashore is likewise violation of law. So is the hawking of such salt. In short, you may choose any one of these devices to break the salt monopoly."

This is just the first part of the speech, but it clearly outlines all that Gandhi expected from his supporters and what they can expect from him. The sender, message, and recipient are aligned. Because of the clarity in the way Gandhi communicated with his audience and followers, the Salt March was one of his most successful campaigns against British rule in India.

Good communication yields good results.

FINAL WORDS

Communication remains an aspect of our lives that we continuously have to learn and refine to effectively live in peace and harmony with each other. As John Powel so aptly put it:

"Communication works for those who work at it."

This book has highlighted all aspects of communication, from verbal to written and body language cues. These are components of communication that make it easier to not only understand each other but to work and live together.

Our approach to communication is ever-evolving, and we have to keep up with the evolution to be effective in our personal and professional lives. Remind yourself of all the things you have learned in this book as you communicate with others, including

- Overcoming learned helplessness
- Turning on your awareness
- Growing your empathy
- Looking out for body language
- Listening rather than hearing
- Taking and giving feedback.

With the help of this book, we can look forward to continuing momentum on our communication journey!

If you enjoyed the book, I would be incredibly thankful if you could take just 60 seconds to write a brief review on Amazon, even if it's just a few sentences. Your communication helps me create even better content for you.

A FREE GIFT TO THE READERS

Thank you for reading *The Effective Communication Method*.
I hope you will find it insightful and practical.
To help you get the best results I have included the following additional
material that no extra cost to you:

This is a quick guide to managing your emotions that plays an
important role in communications.
To get your additional material please scan the QR code below:

REFERENCES

Benjamin, K. (2012, September 12th) "Historical Geniuses and their Psychiatric Conditions." https://www.theatlantic.com/health/archive/2012/09/historical-geniuses-and-their-psychiatric-condi tions/262249/

Cherry, K. (2020, July, 19th). "What Is the Unconscious?" https://www.verywellmind.com/what-is-the-unconscious-2796004

Cuncic, A. (2021, May 11th). "What is Defensiveness?" https://www.verywellmind.com/what-is-defensiveness-5115075

Gowmon, V. (2019). "4 Keys to Conscious Communication" https://www.vincegowmon.com/4-keys-to-conscious-communication/

Landrum, S. (2015, July, 20th), 10 Secrets to Sounding Confident." https://www.fastcompany.com/3048748/10-secrets-to-sounding-confident

Johnson, R. (2022, May 8th). What is Language? The 5 Basic Elements of Language Defined." https://owlcation.com/humanities/What-is-Language-The-Five-Basic-Elements-of-Language-Defined

Johnson, R, Johnson N. (2016, october, 10th) " How to Overcome Your fear of Public Speaking" https://www.britishcouncil.org/voices-magazine/how-overcome-fear-public-speaking

Manik, S. "Function of Language As Found in Economical News." https://uhn.ac.id/files/akademik_files/1712070220_2015_The%20Episteme%20Journal%20of%20Linguistics%20and%20Litera ture%20Vol%201%20No%202_3-Function%20Of%20Language%20As%20Found%20In%20Economical%20News.pdf

Montopoli, J. (2017, February, 20th) "Public Speaking Anxiety and Fear of Brain Freezes." https://nationalsocialanxietycenter.com/2017/02/20/public-speaking-and-fear-of-brain-freezes/

Moore, D (2013, August 19th). Top 10 Symbols Used by More than One Group." https://www.toptenz.net/top-10-symbols-used-by-more-than-one-group.php

Pasaribu, T. "The Analysis of Language Style on the Campaign Speech of Barack Obama." https://uhn.ac.id/files/akademik_files/1712070149_2014_The%20Episteme%20Journal%20of%20Linguistics%20and%20Literature%20Vol%201%20No%201_2-The%20Analysis%20Of%20Language%20Style%20On%20The%20Campaign%20Speech%20Of.pdf

Perry, D. (2020, January 27th). "Writing Styles." "https://web.uri.edu/graduate-writing-center/writing-styles/

Saeed, K. (2017, October 1) "How to Reverse Learned Helplessness." https://psychcentral.com/blog/liberation/2017/10/successfully-overcoming-learned-helplessness-with-learned-optimism#Overcoming-Learned-Helplessness-with-Learned-Optimism

SPLC. (2021). "Ku Klux Klan." https://www.splcenter.org/fighting-hate/extremist-files/ideology/ku-klux-klan

Thakore, K. (2020, August, 7th). "Conscious Communication:- A guide to emotional wellbeing." https://www.krutithakore.com/blog/conscious-communication-a-guide-to-emotional-wellbeing

The Center for Hyperhidrosis. (2020, April, 27th) "Signs of Nervousness & Nervousness Body Language." https://www.hyperhidrosiscumc.com/signs-of-nervousness-nervousness-body-language/

Van Edwards, V. "26 Head Body Language Gestures to Get You A-head of the Game." https://www.scienceofpeople.com/head-body-language/

Van Edwards, V. "Feet Behavior - The Untapped Body Language You Should Know." https://www.scienceofpeople.com/feet-body-language/

Watson, E. (2017). "Pepsi CEO Finally Speaks On Controversial Kendall Jenner Ad." https://www.okayplayer.com/culture/pepsi-ceo-finally-speaks-on-controversial-kendall-jenner-black-lives-matter-ad.html

Printed in the USA
CPSIA information can be obtained
at www.ICGtesting.com
LVHW061814130823
755093LV00005B/393

9 781738 866403